Corporate Tax Statistics
2023

OECD
BETTER POLICIES FOR BETTER LIVES

Please cite this publication as:
OECD (2023), *Corporate Tax Statistics 2023*, OECD Publishing, Paris, https://doi.org/10.1787/f1f07219-en.

ISBN 978-92-64-73206-3 (print)
ISBN 978-92-64-43499-8 (pdf)
ISBN 978-92-64-67141-6 (HTML)
ISBN 978-92-64-89561-4 (epub)

Corporate Tax Statistics
ISSN 2958-485X (print)
ISSN 2958-4434 (online)

Photo credits: Cover © Shutterstock.com.

Corrigenda to OECD publications may be found on line at: www.oecd.org/about/publishing/corrigenda.htm.

Foreword

This is the fifth edition of *Corporate Tax Statistics*, an annual publication that brings together information on corporate taxation and base erosion and profit shifting (BEPS) practices that previously were unavailable to tax policy researchers and policymakers. This includes data on corporate tax rates, revenues, effective tax rates (ETR), tax incentives for research and development (R&D) and innovation, and withholding taxes amongst other data series. *Corporate Tax Statistics* also includes anonymised and aggregated Country-by-Country Report (CbCR) data providing an overview on the global tax and economic activities of thousands of multinational enterprise groups operating worldwide. *Corporate Tax Statistics* follows on from the OECD/G20 BEPS Project and its package of fifteen measures adopted in 2015 to address tax avoidance. The project's Action 11 noted that the lack of available and high-quality data on corporate taxation is a major limitation to the measurement and monitoring of the scale of BEPS and the impact of the measures agreed to be implemented under the OECD/G20 BEPS Project.

The report is structured as follows. Chapter 1 presents internationally comparable data on the tax revenues of OECD, Latin American and the Caribbean (LAC), African, and Asian and Pacific jurisdictions. Chapter 2 contains information on the headline tax rate faced by corporations and can be used to compare the standard tax rate on corporations across jurisdictions and over time. Chapter 3 presents "forward-looking" ETRs, which are synthetic tax policy indicators calculated using information about specific tax policy rules to assess the impact of taxation on returns to a hypothetical investment project. Chapter 4 describes several indicators of R&D tax incentives that offer a complementary view to the standard ETRs in Chapter 3 with a focus on tax support provided through expenditure-based R&D tax incentives.

Chapter 5 contains information on the number of jurisdictions implementing BEPS Action 13, an outcome of the OECD/G20 BEPS Project. As part of BEPS Action 13, CbCR was introduced to support jurisdictions in combating BEPS. An overview of the aggregated and anonymised CbCR data is also provided in Chapter 5, including general data characteristics, limitations of the CbCR data and some general observations from the CbCR data. Chapter 6 includes information on intellectual property (IP) regimes. Chapter 7 presents information on standard and treaty-based withholding taxes (WHTs) which are levied on businesses when they make payments to other foreign or domestic business entities or individuals, e.g., in the form of dividends, interest, and royalties.

This publication was prepared under the auspices of the Working Party No. 2 on Tax Policy and Statistics of the Inclusive Framework on BEPS. The authors wish to thank delegates of Working Party No 2 for their time in preparing the statistics for publication. The publication is led by Ruairi Sugrue, under the supervision of Pierce O'Reilly. Chapters 1 and 2 were prepared by Ruairi Sugrue. Chapters 3 and 4 were prepared by Clara Gascon, Idann Gidron and Ana Cinta Gonzalez Cabral, with input from Silvia Appelt and Fernando Galindo-Rueda. Chapter 5 was prepared by Ruairi Sugrue, Felix Hugger and Idann Gidron. Chapter 6 was prepared by Ruairi Sugrue with input from Jessica De Vries and the Forum for Harmful Tax Practices (FHTP). Chapters 8 and 9 were prepared by Clara Gascon, Idann Gidron, Pierce O'Reilly and Ruairi Sugrue.

Table of contents

FIGURES

TABLES

Reader's guide

Overview

In developing this 2023 edition of the *Corporate Tax Statistics* database, the OECD has worked closely with members of the Inclusive Framework (IF) on base erosion and profit shifting (BEPS) and other jurisdictions willing to participate in the collection and compilation of statistics relevant to corporate taxation.

This database is intended to assist in the study of corporate tax policy and expand the quality and range of data available for the analysis of base erosion and profit shifting. The *Measuring and Monitoring BEPS, Action 11 - 2015 Final Report* highlighted that the lack of quality data on corporate taxation is a major limitation to the measurement and monitoring of the scale of BEPS and the impact of the OECD/G20 BEPS project. While this database is of interest to policy makers from the perspective of BEPS, its scope is much broader. Apart from BEPS, corporate tax systems are important more generally in terms of the revenue that they raise and the incentives for investment and innovation that they create. The *Corporate Tax Statistics* database[1] brings together a range of information to support the analysis of corporate taxation, in general, and of BEPS, in particular.

The database compiles new data items as well as statistics in various existing data sets held by the OECD. The fourth edition of the database contains the following categories of data:

- Corporate tax revenues;
- Statutory corporate income tax (CIT) rates;
- Corporate effective tax rates;
- Tax incentives for research and development (R&D);
- Action 13 implementation;
- Anonymised and aggregated statistics collected via Country-by-Country Reports;
- Intellectual property regimes;
- Standard withholding tax rates;
- Bilateral tax treaties.

Box 1. *Corporate tax statistics* database

Corporate tax revenues:

- data are from the OECD's Global Revenue Statistics Database;[1]
- covers 120 jurisdictions from 1965-2020 (for OECD members) and 1990-2020 (for non-OECD members);

Statutory CIT rates:

- covers all IF jurisdictions from 2000-2023;

Standard withholding tax rates:

- data covering 119 jurisdictions from 2022 – 2023;

Corporate effective tax rates:

- covers 77 jurisdictions for 2017-2022;

Tax incentives for R&D:

- two indicators produced by the Centre for Tax Policy and Administration and the OECD Directorate for Science, Technology and Innovation;
  - covers 48 jurisdictions for 2019-2022 (for preferential tax treatment for R&D, based on effective average tax rates and cost of capital for R&D);
- data are from the OECD R&D Tax Incentive Database[2] produced by the OECD Directorate for Science, Technology and Innovation;
  - covers 49 jurisdictions for 2000-2020 (for tax and direct government support as a percentage of R&D);
  - covers 49 jurisdictions for 2000-2022 (for implied subsidy rates for R&D, based on the B-Index);

Action 13 implementation:

- information on the implementation of the minimum standard on Country-by-Country Reporting

Anonymised and aggregated CbCR statistics:

- data are from anonymised and aggregated CbCR statistics prepared by OECD Inclusive Framework members and submitted to the OECD;
- covers 52 jurisdictions for 2016-2020;

Intellectual property (IP) regimes:

- data collected for 2018-2023 by the OECD's Forum on Harmful Tax Practices;
- covers 61 regimes in 46 jurisdictions for 2023.

Notes:

1. https://www.oecd.org/tax/tax-policy/global-revenue-statistics-database.htm.
2. https://www.oecd.org/fr/innovation/incitations-fiscales-RD-innovation/.

Abbreviations and acronyms

ACE	Allowance For Corporate Equity
BEPS	Base Erosion and Profit Shifting
BERD	Business Expenditure On R&D
CbCR	Country-By-Country Reporting
CIT	Corporate Income Tax
ETR	Effective Tax Rate
EATR	Effective Average Tax Rate
EMTR	Effective Marginal Tax Rate
FDI	Foreign Direct Investment
FHTP	Forum On Harmful Tax Practices
GDP	Gross Domestic Product
GTARD	Government Tax Relief for Business R&D
ICAP	International Compliance Assurance Programme
IF	Inclusive Framework On BEPS
IP	Intellectual Property
LAC	Latin American and The Caribbean
MNE	Multinational Enterprise
NPV	Net Present Value
R&D	Research And Development
RPR	Related Party Revenues

SMEs	Small And Medium-Sized Enterprises
STR	Statutory Tax Rate
TREAT	CbCR Tax Risk Evaluation and Assessment Tool
UPE	Ultimate Parent Entity
UPR	Unrelated Party Revenues
WHTs	Withholding Taxes

Table 1.1. Names and ISO codes of jurisdictions covered

ISO Code	Name	Iso Code	Name	ISO Code	Name
ALB	Albania	GAB	Gabon	NZL	New Zealand
AND	Andorra	GEO	Georgia	NIC	Nicaragua
AGO	Angola	DEU	Germany	NER	Niger
AIA	Anguilla	GHA	Ghana	NGA	Nigeria
ATG	Antigua And Barbuda	GIB	Gibraltar	MKD	North Macedonia
ARG	Argentina	GRC	Greece	NOR	Norway
ARM	Armenia	GRL	Greenland	OMN	Oman
ABW	Aruba	GRD	Grenada	PAK	Pakistan
AUS	Australia	GTM	Guatemala	PAN	Panama
AUT	Austria	GGY	Guernsey	PNG	Papua New Guinea
AZE	Azerbaijan	GUY	Guyana	PRY	Paraguay
BHS	Bahamas	HTI	Haiti	PER	Peru
BHR	Bahrain	HND	Honduras	PHL	Philippines
BGD	Bangladesh	HKG	Hong Kong, China	BOL	Plurinational State of Bolivia
BRB	Barbados	HUN	Hungary	POL	Poland
BEL	Belgium	ISL	Iceland	PRT	Portugal
BLZ	Belize	IND	India	QAT	Qatar
BEN	Benin	IDN	Indonesia	COG	Republic of the Congo
BMU	Bermuda	IRL	Ireland	ROU	Romania
BTN	Bhutan	IMN	Isle Of Man	RWA	Rwanda
BIH	Bosnia And Herzegovina	ISR	Israel	KNA	Saint Kitts And Nevis
BWA	Botswana	ITA	Italy	LCA	Saint Lucia
BRA	Brazil	JAM	Jamaica	VCT	Saint Vincent and the Grenadines
VGB	British Virgin Islands	JPN	Japan	WSM	Samoa
BRN	Brunei Darussalam	JEY	Jersey	SMR	San Marino
BGR	Bulgaria	JOR	Jordan	SAU	Saudi Arabia
BFA	Burkina Faso	KAZ	Kazakhstan	SEN	Senegal
CPV	Cabo Verde	KEN	Kenya	SRB	Serbia
KHM	Cambodia	SWZ	Eswatini, Kingdom of	SYC	Seychelles
CMR	Cameroon	KOR	Korea	SLE	Sierra Leone
CAN	Canada	KGZ	Kyrgyzstan	SGP	Singapore
CYM	Cayman Islands	LAO	Lao People's Democratic Republic	SVK	Slovak Republic
TCD	Chad	LVA	Latvia	SVN	Slovenia
CHL	Chile	LSO	Lesotho	SLB	Solomon Islands
CHN	China	LBR	Liberia	ZAF	South Africa
COL	Colombia	LIE	Liechtenstein	ESP	Spain
COK	Cook Islands	LTU	Lithuania	LKA	Sri Lanka
CRI	Costa Rica	LUX	Luxembourg	SWE	Sweden
CIV	Côte D'Ivoire	MAC	Macau, China	CHE	Switzerland

HRV	Croatia	MDG	Madagascar	THA	Thailand
CUB	Cuba	MWI	Malawi	TGO	Togo
CUW	Curaçao	MYS	Malaysia	TKL	Tokelau
CZE	Czechia	MDV	Maldives	TTO	Trinidad And Tobago
COD	Democratic Republic of The Congo	MLI	Mali	TUN	Tunisia
DNK	Denmark	MLT	Malta	TUR	Türkiye
DJI	Djibouti	MRT	Mauritania	TCA	Turks And Caicos Islands
DMA	Dominica	MUS	Mauritius	UGA	Uganda
DOM	Dominican Republic	MEX	Mexico	UKR	Ukraine
EGY	Egypt	MCO	Monaco	ARE	United Arab Emirates
SLV	El Salvador	MNG	Mongolia	GBR	United Kingdom
GNQ	Equatorial Guinea	MNE	Montenegro	USA	United States
EST	Estonia	MSR	Montserrat	URY	Uruguay
FRO	Faroe Islands	MAR	Morocco	UZB	Uzbekistan
FJI	Fiji	NAM	Namibia	VUT	Vanuatu
FIN	Finland	NRU	Nauru	VNM	Viet Nam
FRA	France	NLD	Netherlands	ZMB	Zambia

Executive summary

Corporate Tax Statistics **is an annual publication intended to assist in the study of corporate tax policy and expand the quality and range of data available for the analysis of base erosion and profit shifting (BEPS).** This includes data on corporate tax rates, revenues, effective tax rates, and tax incentives for research and development (R&D) and innovation, withholding tax rates, Intellectual Property (IP) regimes, and tax treaties. *Corporate Tax Statistics* also includes anonymised and aggregated Country-by-Country Reporting (CbCR) data providing an overview on the global tax and economic activities of thousands of multinational enterprise groups operating worldwide.

This year's publication includes several expansions to the available data. Two years of CbCR data are provided in this edition, improving the timeliness of the data. The data also include new data in on low-taxed profit globally through an expansion of Table 5 of the CbCR data. A new database of tax treaties is included for the first time, as well as a significant expansion in the coverage of the data on statutory tax rates. The main findings of the report are as follows:

- **Corporate tax revenues continue to make an important contribution to jurisdictions' economies.** In 2020, the share of corporate tax revenues in total tax revenues was 15.1% on average across the 116 jurisdictions for which corporate tax revenues are available in the database, and the share of these revenues as a percentage of Gross Domestic Product (GDP) was 3.0% on average.
- **The data point to a stabilisation of corporate tax rates in recent years.** Statutory corporate income tax (STR) rates remain stable in the period between 2021 and 2023, arresting their long-term decline over the last two decades, though rates remain far below historic averages. The average combined (central and sub-central government) statutory tax rate for all 141 Inclusive Framework jurisdictions declined dramatically from 28.1% in 2000 to 21.3% in 2020. However, it remained at 21.1% in 2021, 2022, and 2023.
- **However, the Effective Average Tax Rate (EATR) has continued to decline modestly in recent years.** Looking at the development of the composite EATR from 2017 and 2022, the unweighted average composite EATR has declined steadily over this period (1.5 p.p.), from 21.7% in 2017 to 20.2% in 2022.
- Some signs of stabilisation of corporate tax rates could also be seen in a stabilization of the tax subsidies being provided for R&D investments in recent years. While R&D incentives can provide important tax support for R&D and innovation, they also often been seen as a means of attracting mobile intangible investment which can be subject to strong competitive pressures. Tax subsidies for R&D have stabilised in recent years, with the average subsidy reducing EATRs for R&D by 34.8% in 2020, 35.3% in 2021 and 34.7% in 2022.
- **This year's CbCR data improve the timeliness of the series substantially.** The 2023 release of anonymised and aggregated CbCR data contains two years of data (for financial years 2019 and 2020) in a significant step towards increased timeliness of CbCR data. It includes aggregated data on the activities of almost 7 600 multinational enterprises (MNEs) worldwide.

- The data continues to point to the existence of base erosion and profit shifting, which highlights the importance of implementing the international tax agreement. Data for Fiscal Years 2019 and 2020 continues to show a misalignment between the location where profits are reported and the location where economic activities occur. The new CbCR data show that the median value of revenues per employee in investment hubs is USD 1 710 000 as compared to just USD 290 000 for all other jurisdictions. While these effects could reflect some commercial considerations, they are also likely to indicate the existence of BEPS practices.
- **The report contains new data on low-taxed profit worldwide.** For the first time, the report includes a jurisdiction-by-jurisdiction breakdown of low-taxed profit of MNEs (defined as profit taxed at an effective tax rate below 15%) headquartered in some jurisdictions. While not all jurisdictions could provide this breakdown for confidentiality reasons, the new data highlight the presence of low-taxed profit in low-tax and high-tax jurisdictions alike, with more than half of the low-taxed profit in the new data located in jurisdictions with average Effective Tax Rates (ETR) above 15%.
- **Most IP regimes covered in the database have been found to be not harmful by the OECD Forum on Harmful Tax Practices.** Under the Action 5 BEPS peer review process, the OECD Forum on Harmful Tax Practices identified 61 IP regimes in place across 46 jurisdictions in 2023. Forty-three regimes in total were found to be not harmful; 26 of these regimes were found to be not harmful after having been amended to align with the Action 5 minimum standard.
- **The 2023 edition of *Corporate Tax Statistics* continues to expand the data available to study MNE activity.** In addition to the new CbCR data, this years' edition includes the second release of statistics on Withholding Tax rates (WHT), as well as significant increases in the coverage of the ETR and STR series. The dataset consists of tax rates on dividends, interest and royalty payments that are applicable as of the 2023 fiscal year. It also for the first time contains data on WHT tax rates under tax treaties, continuing the expansion of Corporate Tax Statistics to provide additional data to tax researchers and policymakers alike.

Note

[1] www.oecd.org/tax/beps/corporate-tax-statistics-database.htm.

1 Corporate tax revenues

Key insights

- In 2020, the share of corporate tax revenues in total tax revenues was 15.1% on average across the 116 jurisdictions for which corporate tax revenues are available in the database, and the share of these revenues as a percentage of gross domestic product (GDP) was 3.0% on average.
- The size of corporate tax revenues relative to total tax revenues and relative to GDP varies by groupings of jurisdictions. In 2020, corporate tax revenues were a larger share of total tax revenues on average in Africa (19.3% in the 30 jurisdictions), Asia and Pacific (18.8% in the 29 jurisdictions) and Latin American and The Caribbean (LAC) (15.6% in the 27 jurisdictions) than the OECD (9.0%). The average of corporate tax revenues as a share of GDP was the largest in LAC (3.4% in the 27 jurisdictions), followed by Asia and Pacific (3.1% in the 29 jurisdictions), Africa (3.1% in the 30 jurisdictions) and the OECD (2.8%).
- In fifteen jurisdictions – Bhutan, Chad, Egypt, Equatorial Guinea, Ghana, Guyana, Indonesia, Kazakhstan, Liechtenstein, Malaysia, Maldives, Namibia, Nigeria, Singapore and Trinidad and Tobago – corporate tax revenues made up more than one-quarter of total tax revenues in 2020.
- Corporate tax revenues are driven by the economic cycle. For the period 2000-20, average corporate tax revenues as a percentage of GDP reached their peak in 2008 (3.5%) and declined in 2009 and 2010 (3.1% and 3.1% respectively), reflecting the impact of the 2008 global financial and economic crisis.

Data on corporate tax revenues can be used for comparison across jurisdictions and to track trends over time. The data in the Corporate Tax Statistics database is drawn from the OECD's Global Revenue Statistics Database and allows for the comparison of individual jurisdictions as well as average corporate tax revenues across OECD, LAC, African, and Asian and Pacific jurisdictions.[1]

The Corporate Tax Statistics database contains four corporate tax revenue indicators:

- the level of corporate tax revenues in national currency;
- the level of corporate tax revenues in USD;
- corporate tax revenues as a percentage of total tax revenue;
- corporate tax revenues as a percentage of gross domestic product (GDP).

The data are from the OECD's Global Revenue Statistics Database, which presents detailed, internationally comparable data on tax revenues. The classification of taxes and methodology is described in detail in the OECD's Revenue Statistics Interpretative Guide.

Trends in corporate tax revenues

Data from the OECD's *Corporate Tax Statistics* database show that there was a slight increase in both the average of corporate income tax (CIT) revenues as a share of total tax revenues and as a share of GDP between 2000 and 2019 across the 116 jurisdictions for which data are available.[2] Average corporate tax revenues as a share of total tax revenues increased from 12.6% in 2000 to 15.1% in 2020, and average CIT revenues as a percentage of GDP increased from 2.6% in 2000 to 3.0% in 2020.

Between 2000 and 2019, the trend for both indicators is very similar (Figure 1.1). When measured both as a percentage of total tax revenues and as a percentage of GDP, corporate tax revenues reached their peak in 2008 and then dipped in 2009 and 2010, reflecting the impact of the global financial and economic crisis. While average CIT revenues recovered after 2010, the unweighted averages declined in 2014, 2015 and 2016 across all 116 jurisdictions for which data are available. The unweighted averages recovered slightly in 2017 and 2018 as a result of increases across a wide range of jurisdictions. This two-year period of increases was followed by a slight decline in 2019 in both indicators, however in 2020, average CIT revenues as a share of total tax revenues increased slightly while average CIT as a share of GDP continued to decline slightly.

Figure 1.1. Average corporate tax revenues as a percentage of total tax and as a percentage of GDP

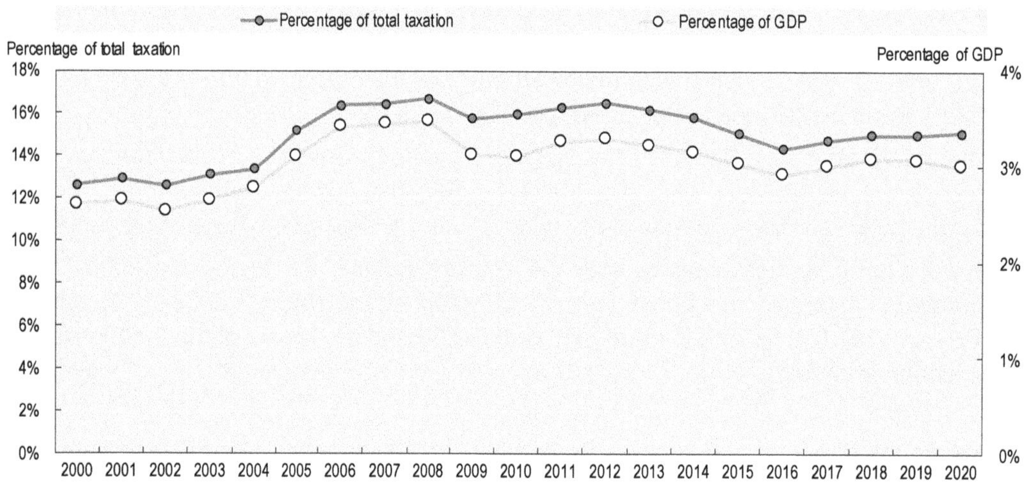

StatLink https://stat.link/cn178d

The averages mask considerable differences across jurisdictions (Figure 1.2). In 2020, jurisdictions differed considerably in the portion of total tax revenues raised by the CIT. In Bhutan, Chad, Egypt, Equatorial Guinea, Ghana, Guyana, Indonesia, Kazakhstan, Liechtenstein, Malaysia, Maldives, Namibia, Nigeria, Singapore and Trinidad and Tobago, CIT revenue accounted for more than 25% of total tax revenue. In Bhutan, Chad and Equatorial Guinea, it accounted for more than 40%. In contrast, some jurisdictions – such as the Bahamas, Estonia, Germany, Greece, Hungary, Italy, Latvia, Nauru, Tokelau, the United States and Vanuatu[3] – raised less than 5% of total tax revenue from the CIT. In most jurisdictions, the difference in the level of corporate taxes as a share of total tax revenues reflects differences in the levels of other taxes raised.

The average revenue share of corporate tax in 2020 also varied across the OECD and the regional groupings (LAC, Asia and Pacific and Africa). In 2020, the OECD average was the lowest, at 9.0%, followed by the LAC average (15.6% in 27 jurisdictions), the Asian and Pacific average (18.8% in 29 jurisdictions) and the African average (19.3% in 30 jurisdictions).

Some of the variation in the share of CIT in total tax revenues results from differences in statutory corporate tax rates, which also vary considerably across jurisdictions. In addition, this variation can be explained by institutional and jurisdiction-specific factors, including:

- the degree to which firms in a jurisdiction are incorporated;
- the breadth of the CIT base;
- the current stage of the economic cycle and the degree of cyclicality of the corporate tax system (for example, from the generosity of loss offset provisions);
- the extent of reliance on other types of taxation, such as taxes on personal income and on consumption;
- the extent of reliance on tax revenues from the exploitation of natural resources;
- other instruments that postpone the taxation of earned profits.

Generally, differences in corporate tax revenues as a share of total tax revenues should not be interpreted as being related to base erosion and profit shifting (BEPS) behaviour, since many other factors are likely to be more significant, although profit shifting may have some effects at the margin.

Corporate tax revenues as a share of GDP

Corporate tax revenues as a percentage of GDP also vary across jurisdictions. In 2020, the ratio of corporate tax revenues to GDP were between 2% and 5% of GDP for a majority of the 116 jurisdictions covered (Figure 1.3). For a few jurisdictions, corporate tax revenues accounted for a larger percentage of GDP; they were more than 5% of GDP in 12 jurisdictions. In contrast, they were less than 2% of GDP in 29 jurisdictions.

In 2020, the OECD and Africa (30 jurisdictions) averages were similar, at 2.9% and 2.8% of GDP respectively, whereas the Asia and Pacific (29 jurisdictions) and LAC (27 jurisdictions) averages were higher (3.1% and 3.4%).

The reasons for the variation across jurisdictions in corporate tax revenues as a percentage of GDP are similar to those that explain why the corporate tax revenue share of total tax revenue differs, such as differences in statutory corporate tax rates and differences in the degree to which firms in a given jurisdiction are incorporated. In addition, the total level of taxation as a share of GDP plays a role. For example, for the 30 African jurisdictions, the relatively high average revenue share of CIT compared to the relatively low average of CIT as a percentage of GDP reflects the low amount of total tax raised as a percentage of GDP (average of 16.0%). Total tax revenue as a percentage of GDP is somewhat higher for the 27 LAC jurisdictions (average of 20.9%), the 29 Asian and Pacific jurisdictions (average of 19.1%) and for the OECD jurisdictions (average of 33.6%). Across jurisdictions in the database, low tax-to-GDP ratios may reflect policy choices as well as other challenges associated with domestic resource mobilisation (e.g., administrative capacity and levels of compliance).

Figure 1.2. Corporate tax revenues as a percentage of total tax revenues, 2020

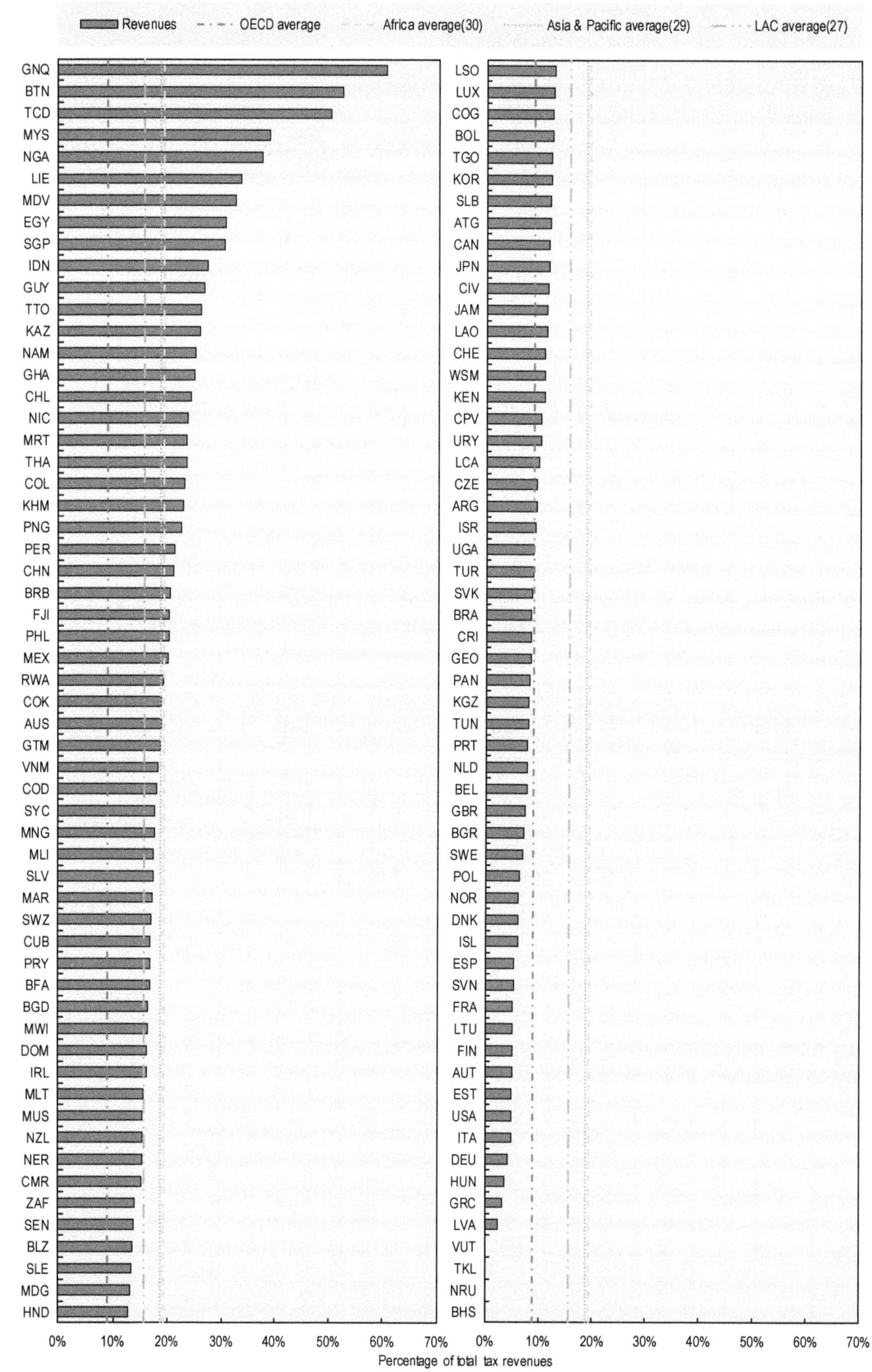

StatLink https://stat.link/l6bc52

Figure 1.3. Corporate tax revenue as a percentage of GDP, 2020

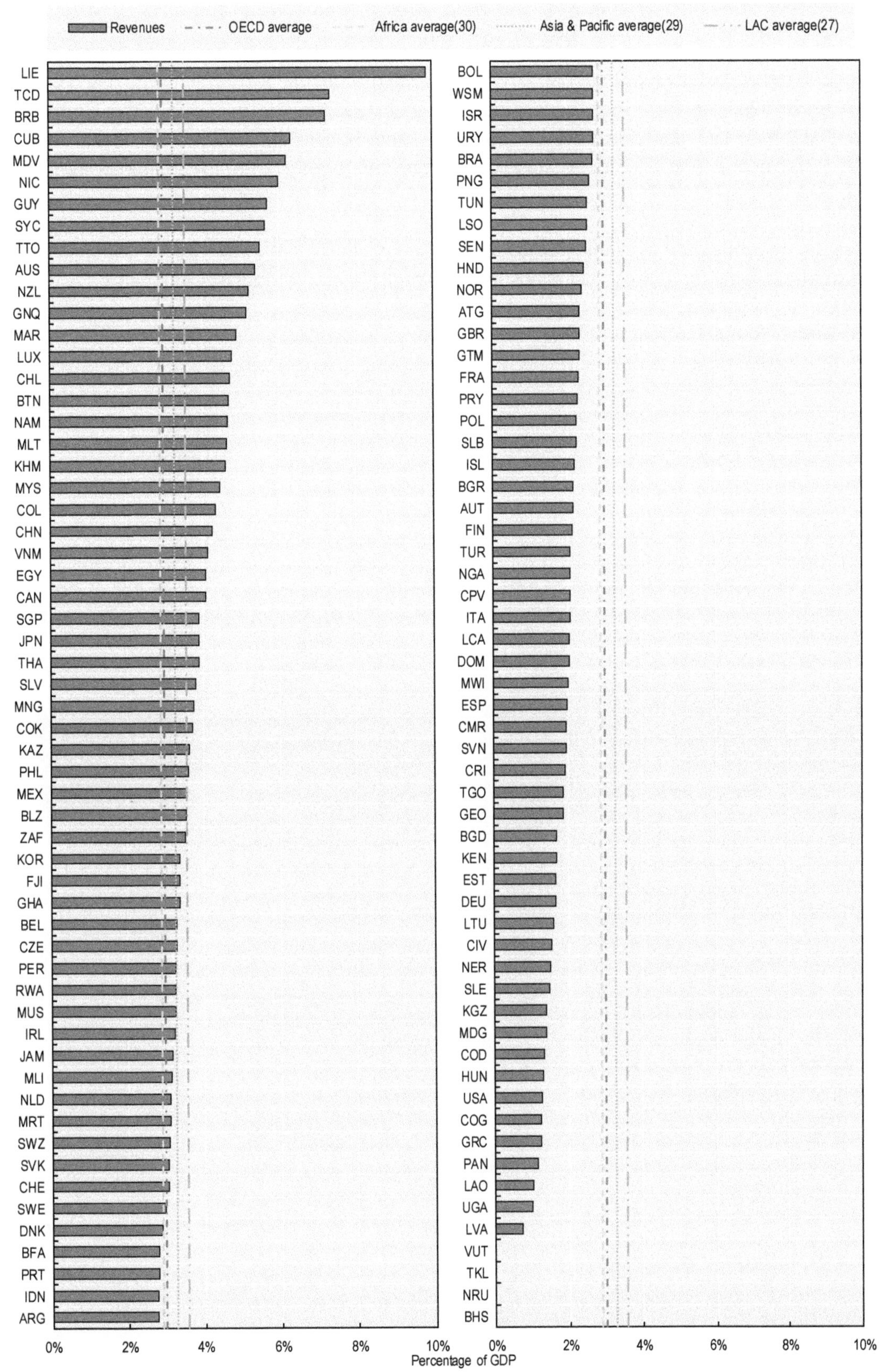

StatLink https://stat.link/sux05w

Notes

[1] The Global Revenue Statistics Database covers 120 jurisdictions as of October 2023. Data on corporate tax revenues is available for 116of these jurisdictions. In addition to the OECD, the Global Revenue Statistics Database also contains data on 29 Asian and Pacific jurisdictions, 27 Latin America and Caribbean jurisdictions, and 30 African jurisdictions, and averages for the LAC, African, and Asian and Pacific regions.

[2] The latest tax revenue data available across all jurisdictions in the database are for 2020, although there are 2021 data available for some jurisdictions in the Global Revenue Statistics database.

[3] The Bahamas, Nauru, Tokelau and Vanuatu do not levy a corporate income tax.

2 Statutory corporate income tax rates

Key insights

- Statutory corporate income tax (CIT) rates have been decreasing on average over the last two decades, although considerable variation among jurisdictions remains. The average combined (central and sub-central government) STRs for all covered jurisdictions was 21.1% in 2023, compared to 28.2% in 2000.
- Of the 141 jurisdictions covered in the 2023 data, 27 had corporate tax rates equal to or above 30% in 2023, with Colombia and Malta having the highest corporate tax rate at 35.0%.[1]
- In 2023, 12 jurisdictions had no corporate tax regime or a CIT rate of zero. Two jurisdictions, Barbados (5.5%) and Hungary (9%), had a positive corporate tax rate less than 10%. Hungary, however, also has a local business tax, which does not use corporate profits as its base. This is not included in Hungary's statutory tax rate, but it does mean that businesses in Hungary are subject to a higher level of tax than its statutory tax rate (STR) reflects.
- Comparing corporate tax rates between 2000 and 2023, 111 jurisdictions had lower tax rates in 2023, while 15 jurisdictions had the same tax rate, and 15 had higher tax rates (Andorra; Benin; Chile; the Cook Islands; Djibouti; Dominica; Honduras; Hong Kong, China; Jordan; the Maldives; Mongolia; Mauritania; Oman and Papua New Guinea).
- The largest increases between 2000 and 2023 were in Benin (30 percentage points (p.p.)) and Togo (27 p.p.). Benin and Togo did not previously have a corporate tax regime and introduced one during this time period.
- Comparing 2000 and 2023, 14 jurisdictions – Aruba, Barbados, Belize, Bosnia and Herzegovina, Bulgaria, Democratic Republic of the Congo, Germany, Gibraltar, Guernsey, India, Isle of Man, Jersey[2], Paraguay and Tunisia – decreased their corporate tax rates by 20 p.p. or more. During this time, Guernsey, Jersey and the Isle of Man eliminated preferential regimes and reduced their standard corporate tax rates to zero and Barbados reduced its standard corporate tax rate to 5.5% after eliminating its preferential regime.
- From 2022 to 2023, the combined STR decreased in four jurisdictions (Aruba, Austria, Korea and St. Vincent and the Grenadines) and there were four increases across the 141 jurisdictions covered (Morocco, Sri Lanka, Türkiye and the United Kingdom).
- The jurisdictions with the largest decreases in the combined corporate tax rate between 2022 and 2023 were Aruba and Türkiye (both decreasing by 3 p.p.).

Statutory CIT rates show the headline tax rate faced by corporations and can be used to compare the standard tax rate on corporations across jurisdictions and over time. As STRs measure the marginal tax that would be paid on an additional unit of income, in the absence of other provisions in the tax code, they are often used in studies of base erosion and profit shifting (BEPS) to measure the incentive that firms have to shift income between jurisdictions.

Standard statutory CIT rates, however, do not give a full picture of the tax rates faced by corporations in a given jurisdiction. The standard CIT rate does not reflect any special regimes or rates targeted to certain industries or income types, nor does it take into account the breadth of the corporate base to which the rate applies. Further information, such as the data on effective corporate tax rates and intellectual property (IP) regimes in the *Corporate Tax Statistics* database, is needed to form a more complete picture of the tax burden on corporations across jurisdictions.

The Corporate Tax Statistics database reports statutory tax rates for resident corporations at the:

- central government level;
- central government level exclusive of any surtaxes;
- central government level less deductions for subnational taxes;
- sub-central government level;
- combined (central and sub-central) government level.

The standard rate, which is not targeted at any particular industries or income type, is reported. The top marginal rate is reported if a jurisdiction has a progressive corporate tax system. Other special corporate taxes that are levied on a base other than corporate profits are not included.

Most of the downward movement in tax rates between 2000 and 2023 was to corporate tax rates equal to or greater than 10% and less than 30%. The number of jurisdictions with tax rates equal to or greater than 20% and less than 30% almost tripled from 37 jurisdictions to 100 jurisdictions, and the number of jurisdictions with tax rates equal to or greater than 10% and less than 20% more than quadrupled, from eight to 33 jurisdictions.

Despite the general downward movement in tax rates during this period, the number of jurisdictions with very low tax rates of less than 10% remained fairly stable between 2000 and 2023. There were 16 jurisdictions with tax rates less than 10% in 2000, and 14 below that threshold in 2023.

There has, however, been some movement of jurisdictions into and out of this category, and these movements illustrate how headline STRs do not give a complete picture of the tax burden in a jurisdiction. Between 2005 and 2009, the British Virgin Islands, Guernsey, Jersey[3] and the Isle of Man all moved from corporate tax rates above 10% to zero corporate tax rates. In all of these cases, however, before changing their standard corporate tax rate to zero, they had operated broadly applicable special regimes that resulted in very low tax rates for qualifying companies. Meanwhile, Andorra and the Maldives instituted corporate tax regimes and moved from zero rates to positive tax rates (10% in Andorra beginning in 2012 and 15% in the Maldives beginning in 2011). However, they also introduced preferential regimes as part of their corporate tax systems that offered lower rates to qualifying companies.[4]

Figure 2.1. Statutory corporate income tax rates, 2023

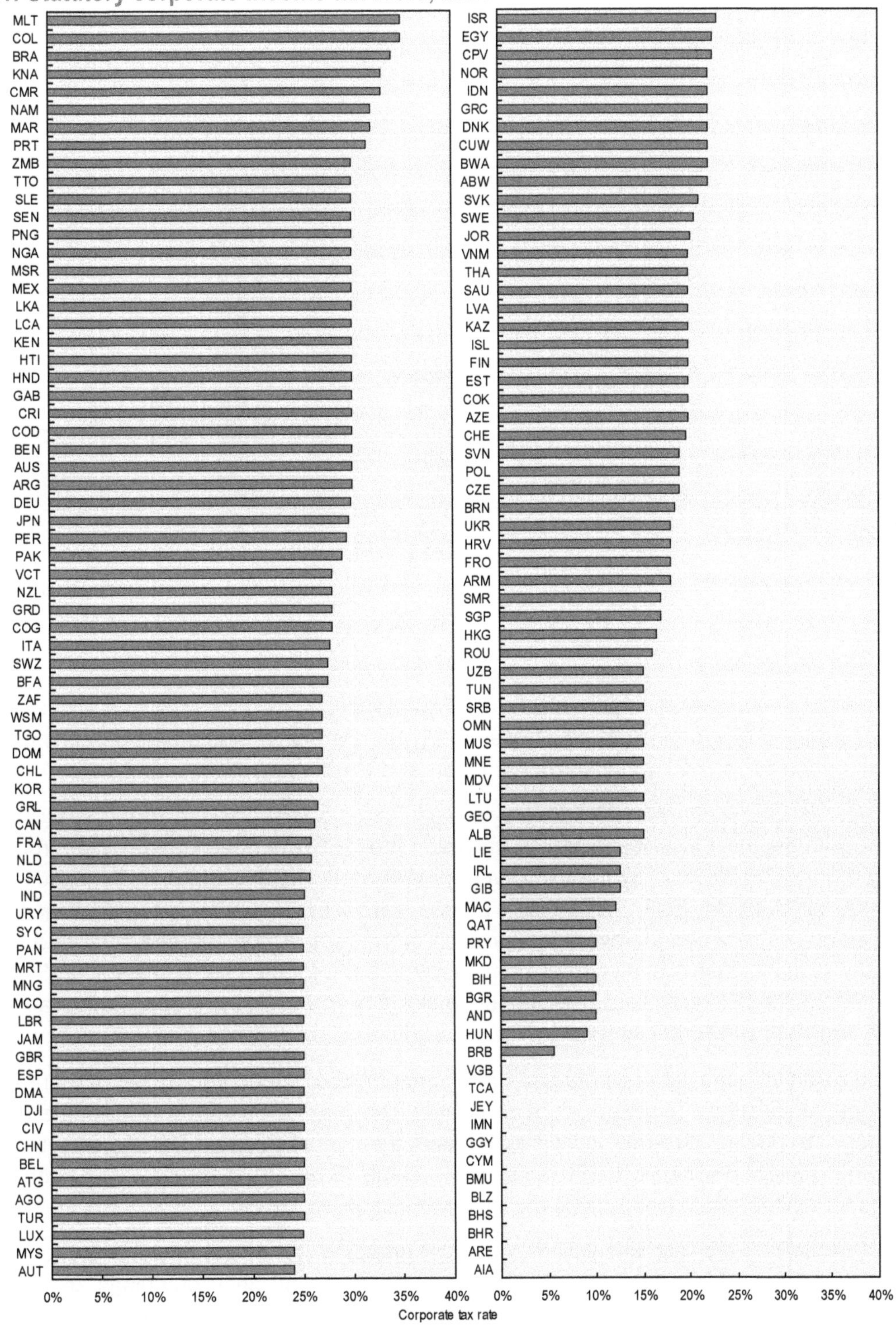

Note: The Kingdom of Saudi Arabia imposes a corporate income tax rate of 20% on a non-Saudi's' share of a resident company or a non-resident's income from a permanent establishment in Saudi Arabia or income of a company operating in the natural gas sector. A higher corporate income tax rate is imposed as well on companies operating in the oil sector (i.e., 50% or higher). The Kingdom of Saudi Arabia also levies the Zakat on companies, which is an example of a tax on both income and equity. The Zakat is levied at 2.5% on a Saudi's share of a resident company (also applies to citizens of Gulf Cooperation Council countries with an established business in the Kingdom of Saudi Arabia), but since it is imposed on income and equity, it yields a higher rate in effective terms. The Saudi government considers the corporate Zakat as an equivalent to corporate income tax, levied on a different basis. It is also considered a covered tax for the purposes of the GloBE rules in the Pillar 2 Blueprint Report (OECD, 2020[1]).

StatLink https://stat.link/sbmte4

Figure 2.2. Changing distribution of corporate tax rates

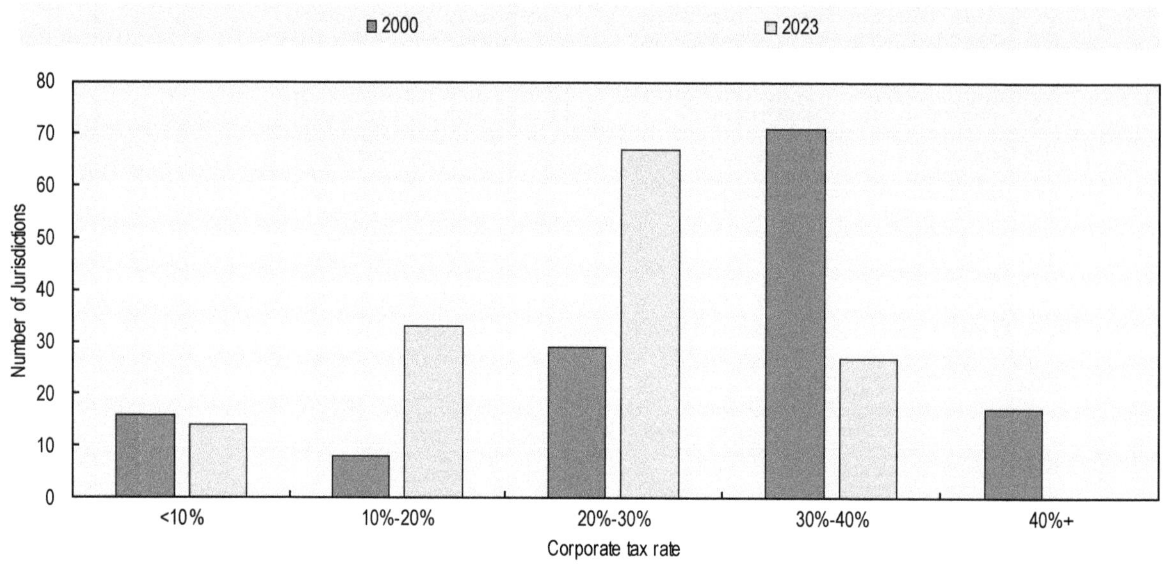

StatLink https://stat.link/a62l0m

Corporate tax rate trends across regions

Since 2000, average STRs have declined across OECD member states and the three regional groupings of jurisdictions considered: African jurisdictions, Asian and Pacific jurisdictions and Latin American and The Caribbean (LAC) jurisdictions Figure 2.3.[5]

The grouping with the most significant decline has been the OECD (a decline of 8.7 p.p., from 32.3% in 2000 to 23.6% in 2023) followed by the LAC average with a decline of 6.6 p.p. in 35 jurisdictions, from 27.9% in 2000 to 21.3% in 2023. While the averages have fallen for each grouping over this period, significant differences between the averages for each group remain: the average corporate tax rate for Africa was 26.7% in 27 jurisdictions in 2023, compared to 23.6% for the OECD, 21.3% in 35 jurisdictions for LAC and 20.2% for 33 jurisdictions in Asia and Pacific. In recent years, averages have stabilised in the OECD, LAC, and Asia and Pacific groupings.

The inclusion of jurisdictions with corporate tax rates of zero affects the average tax rate and has larger effects on some regions than on others, since zero rate jurisdictions are not evenly distributed among the different groups. Excluding zero-rate jurisdictions raises the overall average STR by about 2.7 p.p. per year, while the general downward trend remains the same. From 2000 to 2023, the overall average statutory rate for non-zero rate jurisdictions declined from 31.3% to 23.1%.

The effect of excluding zero-rate jurisdictions varies by grouping. There are no zero-rate jurisdictions in the OECD or 27 African jurisdictions, and so the average STRs of these groupings are not affected. However, three of the 33 Asian and Pacific jurisdictions and five of the 35 LAC jurisdictions have or had statutory corporate tax rates set at zero. Therefore, the average STRs of the 30 Asian and Pacific jurisdictions with positive STRs and the 30 LAC jurisdictions with positive STRs are higher than the averages for those regions when all jurisdictions are included. The average statutory rates of the 30 non-zero-rate Asian and Pacific jurisdictions and the OECD jurisdictions are quite similar over the time period; meanwhile, the average STR for the full group of 33 Asian and Pacific jurisdictions is 4-8 p.p. lower per year than the average STR for OECD jurisdictions. Excluding zero-rate jurisdictions results in the most striking difference in the LAC region. In 2023, the average STR across all 35 LAC jurisdictions (21.3%)

was 5.3 p.p. lower than the average STR for the 30 LAC jurisdictions with positive CIT rates (26.6%). With the exclusion of zero-rate jurisdictions, the average of the remaining 30 LAC jurisdictions is higher than the OECD average and is almost the same as the average statutory rate for the 27 African jurisdictions.

Figure 2.3. Average statutory corporate income tax rates by region

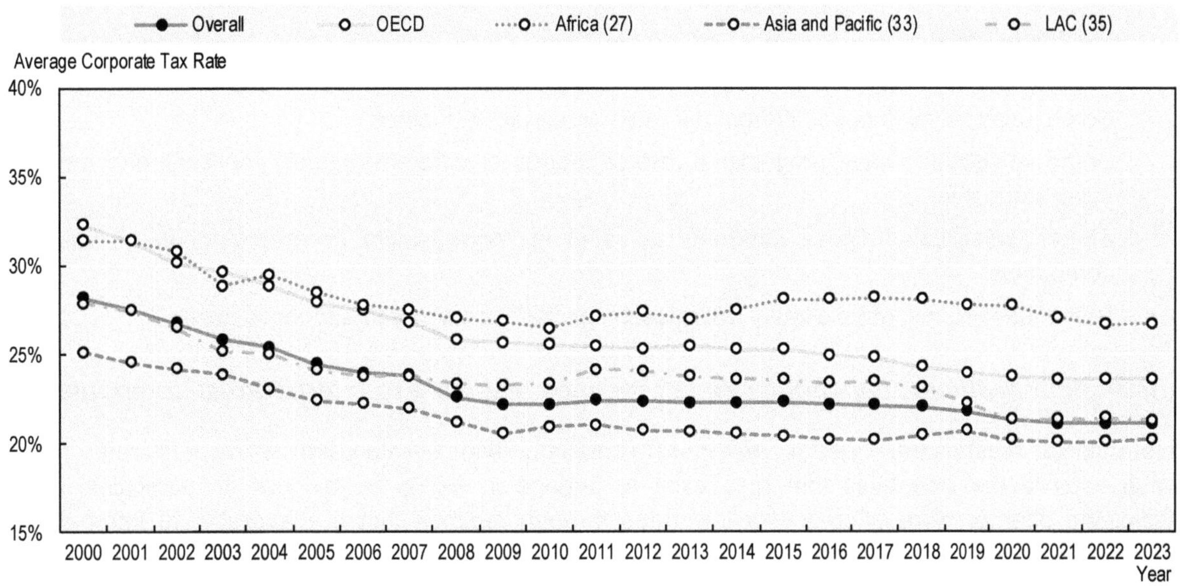

StatLink https://stat.link/xzwamc

Figure 2.4. Average statutory corporate income tax rates by region excluding zero-rate jurisdictions

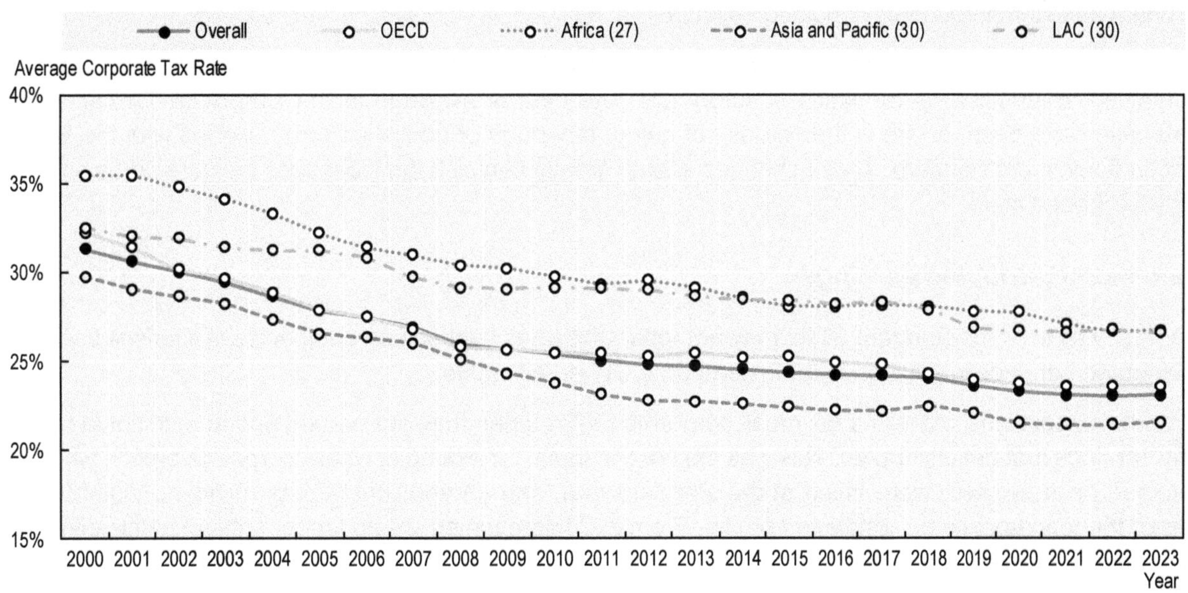

StatLink https://stat.link/x3cqj8

The standard statutory corporate tax rate is not the only corporate tax rate

Standard statutory CIT rates provide a snapshot of the corporate tax rate in a jurisdiction. However, jurisdictions may have multiple tax rates with the applicable tax rate depending on the characteristics of the corporation and the income.

- Some jurisdictions operate preferential tax regimes with lower rates offered to certain corporations or income types.
- Some jurisdictions tax retained and distributed earnings at different rates.
- Some jurisdictions impose different tax rates on certain industries.
- Some jurisdictions have progressive rate structures or different regimes for small and medium sized companies.
- Some jurisdictions impose different tax rates on non-resident companies than on resident companies.
- Some jurisdictions impose lower tax rates in special or designated economic zones.

Jurisdictions with broadly applicable tax regimes available to international companies

Preferential tax regimes are especially important in understanding how standard corporate tax rates do not always capture the incentives that may exist to engage in BEPS behaviours. In particular, some jurisdictions offer or have offered very low rates through regimes that are available to international companies with relatively few restrictions, while maintaining high standard statutory CIT rates.

For example, a number of jurisdictions offer or have offered International Business Companies regimes. Companies qualifying for these regimes pay a reduced rate of tax relative to the standard statutory CIT rate. While that standard STR may be quite high in these jurisdictions, qualifying international business companies were typically exempt from tax or paid tax at a very low rate. There are also special cases, like Malta, which offers a refund of up to six-sevenths of corporate income taxes to both resident and non-resident investors through its imputation system.

Except for the Maltese imputation system, which is not in the scope of the BEPS project, all of the regimes belonging to jurisdictions for which statutory CIT rate data is available in the *Corporate Tax Statistics* database have been, or are in the process of being, amended or abolished to be aligned with the BEPS Action 5 minimum standard. These changes should greatly diminish the incentives these regimes provide for BEPS behaviour.

Taxes on distributed earnings

Another way in which standard STRs may not reflect the rates imposed on companies is if jurisdictions tax distributed earnings in addition to (or instead of) a CIT on all profits.

In some jurisdictions, there is a tax on all corporate profits when they are earned and an additional tax on any earnings that are distributed. This was the case in India, for example, where corporate profits, whether retained or distributed, were taxed at the standard rate, and an additional tax on dividend distributions raised the total tax rate on distributed profits. From 2020 companies are no longer subject to this dividend distribution tax which has led to a large reduction in the statutory CIT rate from 40.6% in 2019 to 25.2% in 2023.

In other jurisdictions, there is no tax on profits when they are earned, and corporate tax is only imposed when profits are distributed. This is the case in Estonia and Latvia, which both tax distributed profits at 20% and impose no tax on retained earnings. While a standard statutory rate of 20% is reported for both jurisdictions in the *Corporate Tax Statistics* database, the rate faced by corporations in these jurisdictions could be much lower and will depend on the proportion of profits that are distributed. In the case of both of these jurisdictions, where a corporation retains all profits and does not pay any dividends in a given period, it will not be subject to any CIT.

References

OECD (2020), *Tax Challenges Arising from Digitalisation – Report on Pillar Two Blueprint: Inclusive Framework on BEPS*, OECD Publishing, Paris, https://doi.org/10.1787/abb4c3d1-en. [1]

Notes

[1] However, Malta offers a refund of up to six-sevenths of corporate income taxes to both resident and non-resident investors through its imputation system. The corporate tax rate in Belize is 40% but as this rate applies only to the petroleum industry, the corporate tax rate in Belize has been included in this database as 0% to ensure consistency of treatment across all jurisdictions.

[2] Jersey's current corporate income tax regime offers bands of 0%, and for certain targeted sectors, 10% and 20%.

[3] Jersey's current corporate income tax regime offers bands of 0%, and for certain targeted sectors, 10% and 20%.

[4] Andorra and the Maldives have recently since amended or abolished their preferential regimes that were not compliant with the BEPS Action 5 minimum standard.

[5] As the sample of jurisdictions for which tax revenue data are available and the sample of jurisdictions for which statutory corporate tax rate data are available are not the same, the average corporate tax revenue and STR data for the different regional groups should not be directly compared.

3 Corporate effective tax rates

Key insights

- Of the 89 jurisdictions covered for 2022, 76 provide accelerated depreciation, meaning that investments in these jurisdictions are subject to Effective Average Tax Rate (EATRs) below their statutory tax rate (STRs). Among those jurisdictions, the average reduction of the STR was 1.9 p.p.; in 2022, the largest reductions were observed in Italy (12.3 p.p.), Mauritius (9.3 p.p.), Malta and the United Kingdom (both 6.2 p.p.), Poland (4 p.p.), Germany and the United States (both 3.5 p.p.). In contrast, fiscal depreciation was decelerated in six jurisdictions, leading to EATRs above the statutory tax rate. Among those jurisdictions, the average difference between the EATR and the STR was 5.3 p.p.; the largest differences between EATRs and STRs were observed in Chile (10.9 p.p.), Botswana (9.3 p.p.) and Argentina (4.9 p.p.).
- Among all 89 jurisdictions, eight jurisdictions had an allowance for corporate equity (ACE): Belgium[1], Cyprus, Italy, Liechtenstein, Malta, Poland, Portugal and Türkiye. Including this provision in their tax code has led to an additional reduction in their EATRs of between 0.2 to 4.5 p.p.[2]
- The average EATR across jurisdictions (20.2%) is 1.3 p.p. lower than the average STR (21.5%). The median EATR is 2.5 p.p. lower (22.4%) than the median STR (24.9%). While more than half of the jurisdictions covered have EATRs between 15% and 28%, several Latin American and The Caribbean (LAC) jurisdictions have EATRs at the higher end of the range due to the decelerating effect of their tax depreciation rules for acquired software (e.g., Argentina, Chile and Mexico).
- Effective marginal tax rates (EMTRs) are among the lowest in jurisdictions with an allowance for corporate equity, i.e., Cyprus, Italy, Liechtenstein, Malta, Poland, Portugal and Türkiye.
- Sixteen jurisdictions have decreased the generosity of their tax depreciation rules, resulting in an increase in their EMTRs in 2022 compared to 2021; the largest increase was observed in Italy (6.1 p.p.).
- Thirteen jurisdictions have increased the generosity of their tax depreciation rules, leading to lower EMTRs in 2022 than in 2021; this group includes Mexico (23.2 p.p. decrease), Kenya (12.6 p.p.), Canada (3.3 p.p.), Luxembourg (2.7 p.p.) and Peru (1.7 p.p.). In addition, the EMTR also fell in 2022 in France, the Seychelles and Türkiye due to decreases in the statutory tax rate.
- Disaggregating the results to the asset level reveals that fiscal acceleration is strongest for investments in buildings and tangible assets. The average EATR across jurisdictions is 19.2% for buildings and 19.4% for tangible assets, lower than the average composite EATR (20.2%), which also includes acquired software and inventories. For the tangible asset category, which covers air, railroad and water transport vehicles, road transport vehicles, computer hardware, industrial machinery and equipment, most of this effect is driven by more generous tax depreciation rules for air, railroad and water transport vehicles, as well as for industrial machinery.

- Investments in acquired software are subject to very different ETRs due to significant variation in tax treatment across jurisdictions. In particular, intangibles are non-depreciable in Botswana, Chile and Czechia, leading to strongly decelerated fiscal depreciation. On the other hand, the most generous treatment for acquired software is observed in Canada, Denmark, Germany, Hong Kong (China), Singapore and the United Kingdom, while Italy provides a specific tax credit for the acquisition of highly digitalised intangible assets such as, among others, acquired software.

Variations in the definition of corporate tax bases across jurisdictions can have a significant impact on the tax liability associated with a given investment. For instance, corporate tax systems differ across jurisdictions with regard to several important features, such as fiscal depreciation rules as well as other tax provisions. To capture the effects of these provisions on corporate tax bases and tax liabilities, it is necessary to go beyond a comparison of statutory corporate income tax (CIT) rates.

The *Corporate Tax Statistics* dataset presents "forward-looking" ETRs, which are synthetic tax policy indicators calculated using information about specific tax policy rules. Unlike "backward-looking" ETRs, they do not incorporate any information about firms' actual tax payments. As described in more detail in Box 3.1, the ETRs reported in *Corporate Tax Statistics* focus on the effects of fiscal depreciation and several related provisions (e.g., allowances for corporate equity, half-year conventions, inventory valuation methods). While this includes fiscal depreciation rules for certain kinds of intangible property, namely acquired software, the effects of expenditure-based R&D tax incentives and intellectual property (IP) regimes are not accounted for in the baseline data discussed in this section. However, the following section presents forward-looking ETRs capturing the effects of R&D tax incentives on R&D investments.

The *Corporate Tax Statistics* database contains four forward-looking tax policy indicators reflecting tax rules as of 1 July for the years 2017-22:

- the effective average tax rate (EATR);
- the effective marginal tax rate (EMTR);
- the cost of capital;
- the net present value of capital allowances as a share of the initial investment.

All four tax policy indicators are calculated by applying jurisdiction-specific tax rules to a prospective, hypothetical investment project. Calculations are undertaken separately for investments in different asset types and sources of financing (i.e., debt and equity). Composite tax policy indicators are computed by weighting over assets and sources of finance. More disaggregated results are also reported in the Corporate Tax Statistics database. This section discusses only results for two indicators: the EMTR and the EATR.

The tax policy indicators are calculated for two different macroeconomic scenarios. Unless noted, the results reported in this publication refer to composite effective tax rates based on the macroeconomic scenario with 3% real interest rate and 1% inflation.

Forward-looking corporate effective tax rates in 2022

Two complementary forward-looking ETRs are typically used for tax policy analysis, capturing incentives at different margins of investment decision making:

- EATRs reflect the average tax contribution a firm makes on an investment project earning above-zero economic profits. This indicator is used to analyse discrete investment decisions between two or more alternative projects (along the extensive margin).

- EMTRs measure the extent to which taxation increases the pre-tax rate of return required by investors to break even. This indicator is used to analyse how taxes affect the incentive to expand existing investments given a fixed location (along the intensive margin).

Effective average tax rates

Figure 3.1 shows the composite EATR for the full database. In most jurisdictions, EATRs diverge from the statutory CIT rate; if fiscal depreciation is generous compared to true economic depreciation or if there are other significant base narrowing provisions, the EATR (and also the EMTR) will be lower than the statutory tax rate, i.e., tax depreciation is accelerated. On the other hand, if tax depreciation does not cover the full effects of true economic depreciation, it is decelerated, implying that the tax base will be larger and effective taxation higher.

To allow comparison with the statutory tax rate, the share of the EATR (in p.p.) that is due to a deceleration of the tax base is shaded in light blue in Figure 3.1; reductions of the STR due to acceleration are transparent. In addition, the reduction in the EATR due to an ACE is indicated as a dotted area.

Comparing the patterns of tax depreciation across jurisdictions shows that most jurisdictions provide some degree of acceleration, as indicated by the transparent bars. The most significant effects being observed in jurisdictions with an ACE, such as Italy, Malta, Poland, Portugal and Türkiye among others, as well as in jurisdictions with larger accelerated depreciation provisions, such as Canada, France, South Africa, the United Kingdom and the United States. While fewer jurisdictions have decelerating tax depreciation rules, the effect of deceleration can become large in jurisdictions where acquired software is non-depreciable (e.g., in Botswana and Chile) or depreciable at a very low rate (e.g., in Argentina and to a lesser extent also in Mexico, Papua New Guinea and Peru).

Between 2017 and 2022, average EATRs have tended to decline. This has partly been driven by the decline in statutory CIT rates. Looking at the development of the composite EATR from 2017 and 2022, the unweighted average composite EATR has declined steadily over this period (1.5 p.p.), from 21.7% in 2017 to 20.2% in 2022. The average STR has declined somewhat less over the same time period (1.1 p.p.), from 22.6% in 2017 to 21.5% in 2022, implying that changes to the corporate tax base have also contributed to the reduction in EATRs as well as reductions in the headline rates.

The distribution of EATRs has slightly shifted downwards between 2017 and 2022. Figure 3.2 shows the evolution of different points of the EATR distribution over time. The median represents the EATR of the jurisdiction that lies in the middle of the distribution, 50% of jurisdictions would have EATRs above this value. The 25th percentile represents the EATR where 25% of the jurisdictions would be below this value, and the 75th represents the EATR where 75% of the jurisdictions would be below this value. The median EATR has dropped from 22.8% in 2017 to 22.4% in 2022, while the top and bottom of the distribution have dropped from 28.3% and 16.8% in 2017 to 26.5% and 15.3% in 2022.

Changes to the distribution of the EATR can be attributed to the decline over time in statutory CIT rates and to various base reforms. The largest changes in the distribution of EATRs are concentrated in 2021. In 2021 the median EATR dropped to 22.3%, from 22.7% in 2020 (a decline of 0.4 p.p.). During this year, several countries implemented significant changes in their CIT systems which can explain the observed downward trend. Some of these related to reductions in statutory CIT rates or the introduction of base narrowing.

Figure 3.1. Effective average tax rate, 2022

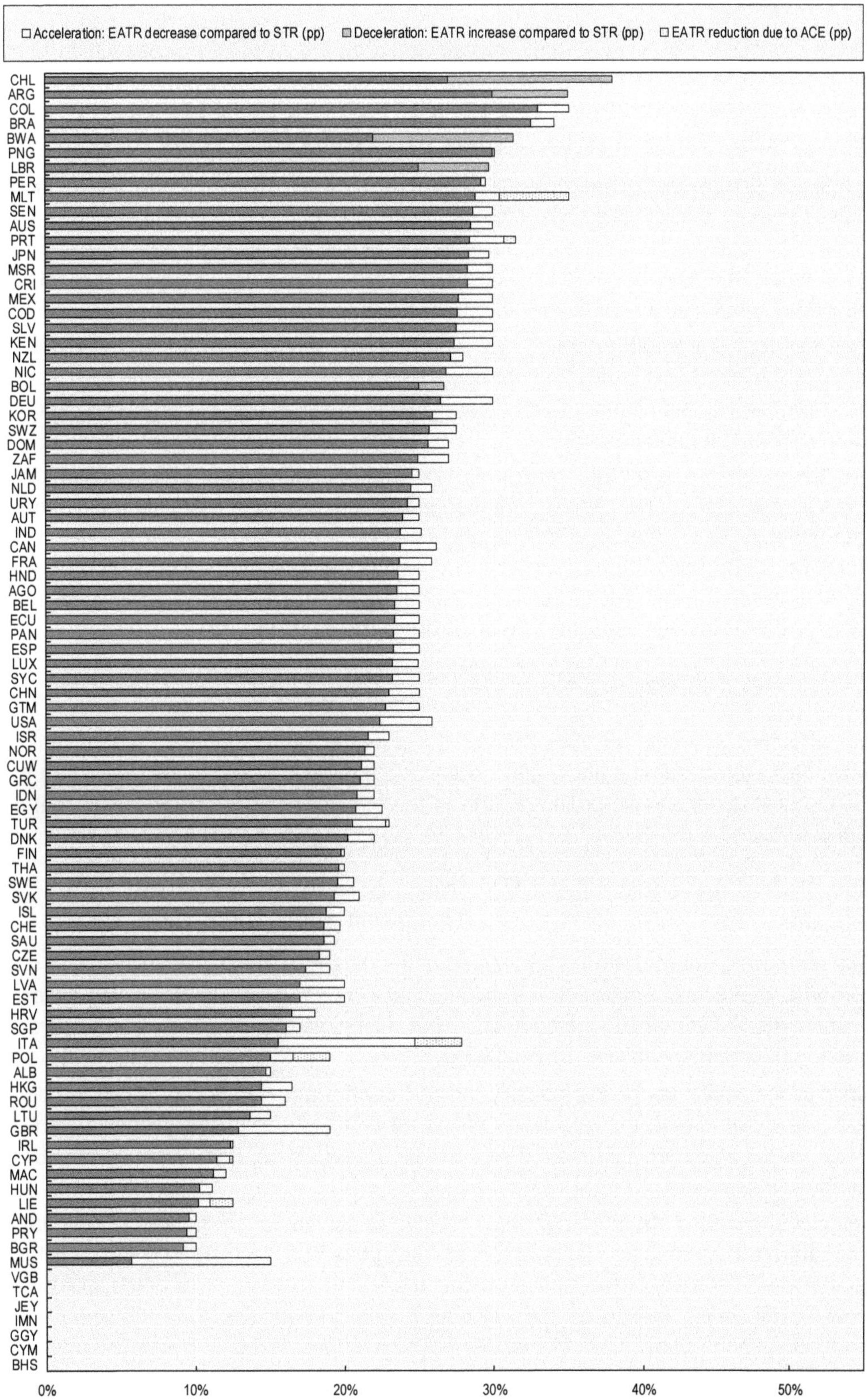

Note: The values of EATRs are calculated assuming a fixed inflation rate at 1% and fixed real interest rate at 3% and setting the rate of return from investments at 0%. Additional parameters are outlined in the Effective Tax Rate (ETR) explanatory annex accompanying Corporate Tax Statistics. https://www.oecd.org/tax/tax-policy/explanatory-annex-corporate-effective-tax-rates.pdf. Note additional details on the modelling of ETRs for Saudi Arabia.[3]

StatLink https://stat.link/x39jni

Box 3.1. Key concepts and methodology

Forward-looking effective tax rates (ETRs) are calculated on the basis of a prospective, hypothetical investment project. The OECD methodology has been described in detail in the OECD Taxation Working Paper No. 38 (Hanappi, 2018[1]), building on the theoretical model developed by Devereux and Griffith (1998[2]; 2003[3]). The methodology builds on the following key concepts:

- **Economic profits** are defined as the difference between total revenue and total economic costs, including explicit costs involved in the production of goods and services as well as opportunity costs such as, for example, revenue foregone by using company-owned buildings or self-employment resources. It is calculated as the net present value (NPV) over all cash flows associated with the investment project.
- **The user cost of capital** is defined as the pre-tax rate of return on capital required to generate zero post-tax economic profits. In contrast, the real interest rate is the return on capital earned in the alternative case, for example, if the investment would not be undertaken and the funds would remain in a bank account.
- **The tax-exclusive effective marginal tax rate** measures the extent to which taxation increases the user cost of capital; it corresponds to the case of a marginal project that delivers just enough profit to break even but no economic profit over and above this threshold. The tax exclusive EMTR uses the real interest rate as the denominator to avoid misspecification at negative values of the cost of capital. Which may arise e.g., due to tax incentives. The tax inclusive EMTR instead uses the cost of capital in the denominator.

$$EMTR = \frac{(Cost\ of\ capital) - (Real\ interest\ rate)}{Real\ interest\ rate}$$

- **The effective average tax rate** reflects the average tax contribution a firm makes on an investment project earning above-zero economic profits. It is defined as the difference in pre-tax and post-tax economic profits relative to the NPV of pre-tax income net of real economic depreciation.

$$EATR = \frac{\left(Economic\ profit_{NPV}^{pre-tax}\right) - \left(Economic\ profit_{NPV}^{post-tax}\right)}{\left(Net\ income_{NPV}^{pre-tax}\right)}$$

- **Real economic depreciation** is a measure of the decrease in the productive value of an asset over time; depreciation patterns of a given asset type can be estimated using asset prices in resale markets. The OECD methodology uses economic depreciation estimates from the US Bureau of Economic Analysis (BEA, 2003[4]).
- Jurisdiction-specific tax codes typically provide **capital allowances** to reflect the decrease in asset value over time in the calculation of taxable profits. If capital allowances match the decay of the asset's value resulting from it being used in production, then fiscal depreciation equals economic depreciation.
- If capital allowances are more generous relative to economic depreciation, fiscal depreciation is **accelerated**; where capital allowances are less generous, fiscal depreciation is referred to as **decelerated**. The NPV of capital allowances, measured as percentage of the initial investment, accounts for timing effects on the value of capital allowances, thus providing comparable information on the generosity of fiscal depreciation across assets and jurisdictions.

The cost of capital, EMTR, EATR as well as the NPV of capital allowances are all available for 89 jurisdictions in the *Corporate Tax Statistics* online database.

Box 3.2. Asset categories and tax provisions covered

The calculations build on a comprehensive coverage of jurisdiction-specific tax rules pertaining to four asset categories.

1. **Buildings** including non-residential structure such as, e.g., manufacturing plants, large engineering structures, office or commercial buildings
2. **Tangible assets** including five specific asset groups: road transport vehicles; air, rail or water transport vehicles; computer hardware; equipment and industrial machinery
3. **Inventories** including, e.g., goods or raw materials in stock
4. **Acquired software** such as computer programmes or applications that a company acquires for commercial purposes

For this edition of *Corporate Tax Statistics*, the data collection process for the tangible asset category has been disaggregated to further improve the cross-country comparability of the ETR data series. Since tangible assets are a particularly broad asset category, collecting disaggregated information on asset-specific tax rules ensures that the variation across specific assets is better captured within this category.

The following corporate tax provisions are covered:

- combined central and sub-central CIT rates;
- asset-specific fiscal depreciation rules, including first-year allowances, half-year or mid-month conventions;
- general tax incentives only if available for a broad group of investments undertaken by large domestic or multinational firms;
- inventory valuation methods including first-in-first-out last-in-first-out and average cost methods;
- allowances for corporate equity.

The composite ETRs reported in this publication are constructed in three steps. First, ETRs are calculated separately for each jurisdiction, asset category and source of finance (debt and equity); within the tangible asset category, ETRs are first calculated separately for each of the five disaggregated assets and then combined through an unweighted average. While the debt-finance case accounts for interest deductibility, jurisdiction-specific limitations to interest deductibility have not been covered in this edition. Second, an unweighted average over the asset categories is taken, separately for both sources of finance. Third, the composite ETRs are obtained as a weighted average between equity- and debt-financed investments, applying a weight of 65% equity and 35% debt finance.

Box 3.3. Macroeconomic scenarios

The two main macroeconomic parameters used in the models, inflation and interest rates, interact with the effects of the tax system in various ways and can have significant effects on ETRs.

The Corporate Tax Statistics database contains ETR results for two different macroeconomic scenarios. In the first scenario, interest and inflation rates are held constant; the second scenario uses jurisdiction-specific macroeconomic parameters. While the former approach addresses the question of how differences in tax systems compare across jurisdictions holding other factors constant, the latter approach gives some indications about the effects of varying macroeconomic conditions on investment incentives as captured by the ETRs.

The results published in this publication build exclusively on the macroeconomic scenario with constant 3% interest and 1% inflation rates, however, results from the other macroeconomic scenario are available in the online database.

Figure 3.2. Changing distribution of corporate effective average tax rates, 2017-2022

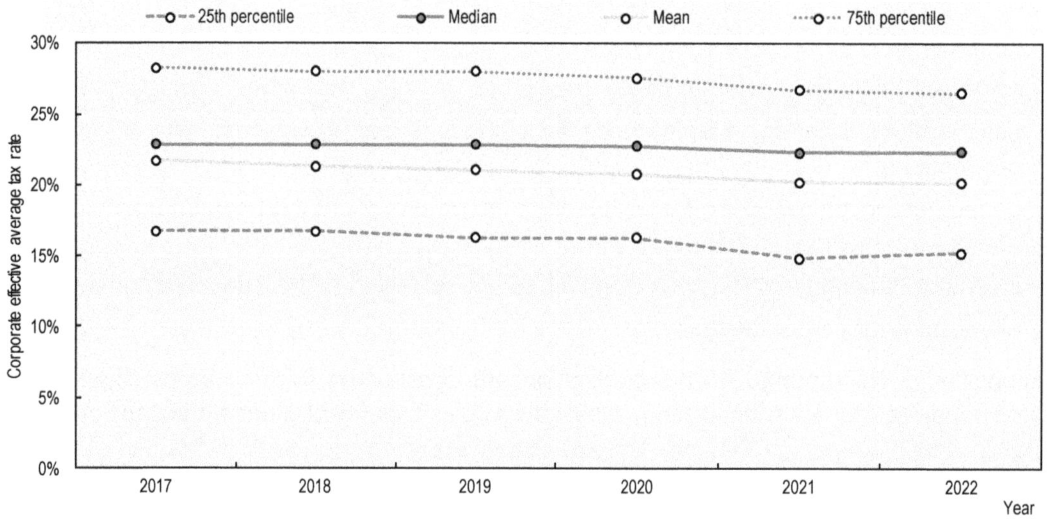

Note: The values of EATRs are calculated assuming a fixed inflation rate at 1% and fixed real interest rate at 3% and setting the rate of return from investments at 0%. Additional parameters are outlined in the ETR explanatory annex accompanying Corporate Tax Statistics. https://www.oecd.org/tax/tax-policy/explanatory-annex-corporate-effective-tax-rates.pdf.

StatLink https://stat.link/9lrza7

Effective marginal tax rates

Figure 3.3 shows the ranking based on the composite EMTR. As highlighted above, the EMTR measures the effects of taxation on the pre-tax rate of return required by investors to break even. While the effects of tax depreciation and macroeconomic parameters work in the same direction as in the case of the EATR, their impacts on the EMTR will generally be stronger because marginal projects do not earn economic profits (see Box 3.1). As a consequence, jurisdictions with relatively high statutory CIT rates and relatively generous capital allowances, notably Italy the United Kingdom and the United States, rank lower than in Figure 3.1. On the other hand, jurisdictions with less generous fiscal depreciation rules, including

Argentina, Japan, New Zealand, Papua New Guinea and Peru (as well as Botswana, Chile, and Czechia), are ranked higher based on the EMTR, as shown in Figure 3.3.

Figure 3.3. Effective marginal tax rate, 2022

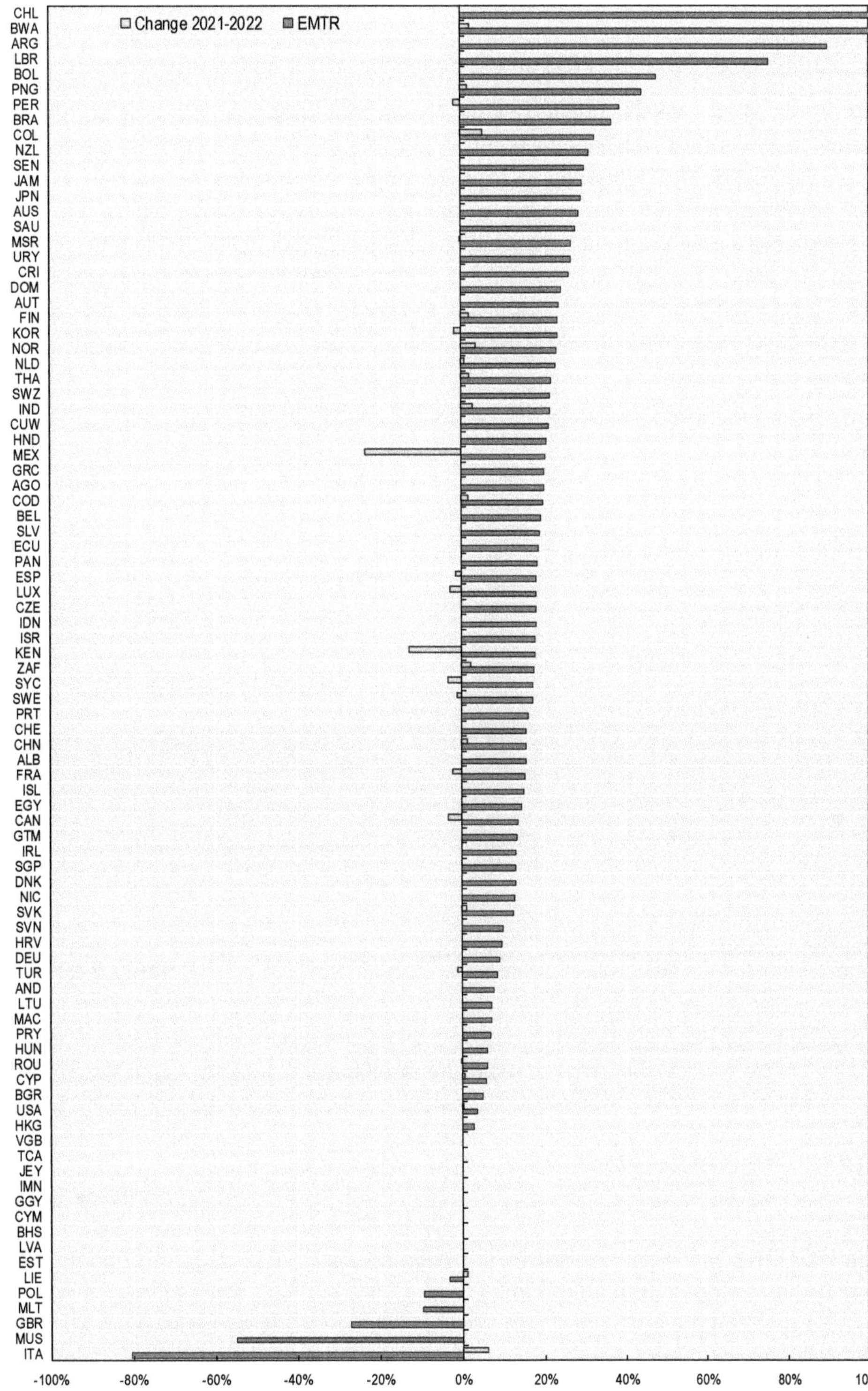

Note: The values of EMTRs are calculated assuming a fixed inflation rate at 1% and fixed real interest rate at 3% and setting the rate of return from investments at 0%. The EMTR is computed using the tax exclusive definition (Box 3.1). Additional parameters are outlined in the ETR explanatory annex accompanying Corporate Tax Statistics. https://oe.cd/5hb.

StatLink https://stat.link/yjesub

If investment projects are financed by debt, it is also possible for the EMTR to be negative, which means that the tax system, notably through interest deductibility, reduces the pre-tax rate of return required to break even and thus enables projects that would otherwise not have been economically viable. Figure 3.3 shows that the composite EMTR, based on a weighted average between equity- and debt-financed projects, is negative in 8 out of 89 jurisdictions; this result is due to the combination of debt finance with comparatively generous tax depreciation rules. For jurisdictions with an ACE, the composite EMTR will generally be lower because of the notional interest deduction available for equity-financed projects.

Comparing EMTRs in 2022 with the previous year shows that changes in the corporate tax provisions covered in the calculations had significant effects on EMTRs in several countries. On the one hand, 16 jurisdictions have decreased the generosity of their tax depreciation rules, resulting in an increase in the EMTRs in 2022 compared to 2021; this group includes Italy (6.1 p.p.), among others. On the other hand, 13 jurisdictions have increased the generosity of their tax depreciation rules, leading to a decrease in their EMTRs in 2022; this group includes Mexico (23.2 p.p. decrease), Kenya (12.6 p.p.), Canada (3.3 p.p.), Luxembourg (2.7 p.p.) and Peru (1.7 p.p.). In addition, the EMTR also fell in 2022 in France, the Seychelles and Türkiye due to decreases in the statutory tax rate.

Figure 3.4. Changing distribution of corporate effective marginal tax rates, 2017-2022

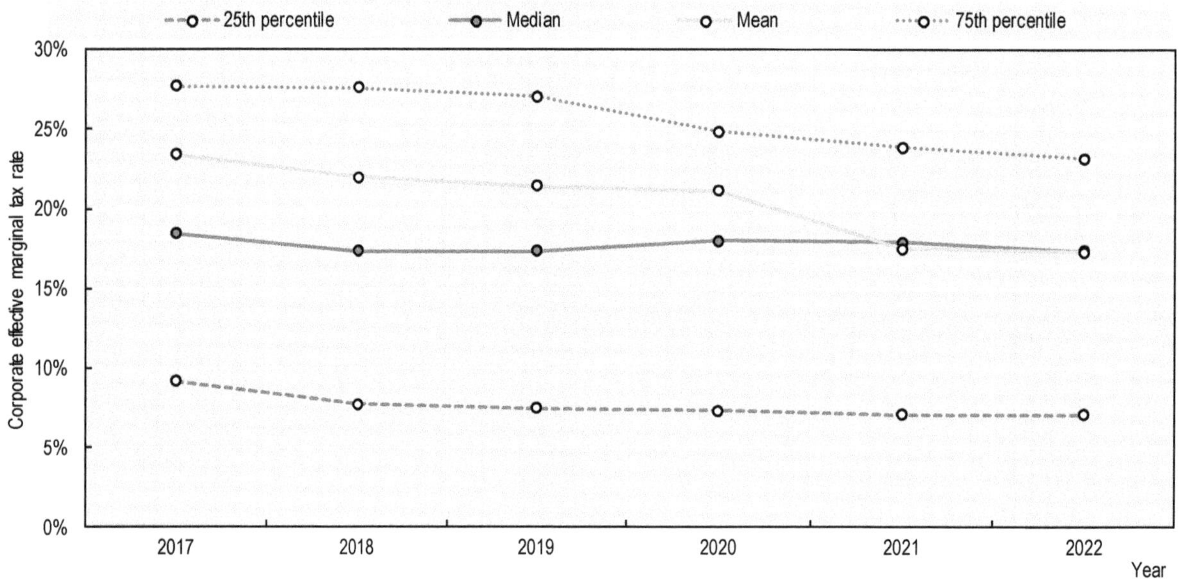

Note: The values of EMTRs are calculated assuming a fixed inflation rate at 1% and fixed real interest rate at 3% and setting the rate of return from investments at 0%. The EMTR is computed using the tax exclusive definition (Box 3.1). Additional parameters are outlined in the ETR explanatory annex accompanying Corporate Tax Statistics. https://www.oecd.org/tax/tax-policy/explanatory-annex-corporate-effective-tax-rates.pdf.

StatLink https://stat.link/7smjp8

The distribution of EMTRs saw a general downward trend between 2017-2022 throughout the distribution. The median EMTR has dropped from 18.4% in 2017 to 17.3% in 2022, while at the top and bottom of the distribution the 75e and 25e percentile dropped from 27.7% and 9.2% respectively in 2017 to 23.2% and 7.1% in 2022.

Effective tax rates by asset categories

The composite ETRs can be further disaggregated by asset categories; jurisdiction-level EATRs and EMTRs by asset categories are available in the online *Corporate Tax Statistics* database. Figure 3.5 summarises these data on ETRs by asset category. The upper panel provides more information on the distribution of asset specific EATRs, comparing them to the distribution of statutory CIT rates. The first vertical line depicts information on the statutory CIT rates; it shows that the mean (i.e., the circle in the middle of the first vertical line) and the median (the light blue triangle) are around 21.4% and 25% respectively, while the 50% of jurisdictions in the middle of the distribution have statutory CIT rates between 18.5% and 27.3%.

The other four vertical lines in the upper panel of Figure 3.5 illustrate the distribution of EATRs across jurisdictions for each of the four asset categories: buildings, tangible assets, inventories and acquired software. Since there is more variation in economic and tax-related characteristics across tangible assets, this category summarises information on investments in several specific tangible assets, i.e., air, railroad and water transport vehicles, road transport vehicles, computer hardware, industrial machinery and equipment (see Box 3.2).

Figure 3.5. EATR and EMTR: Variation across jurisdictions and assets, 2022

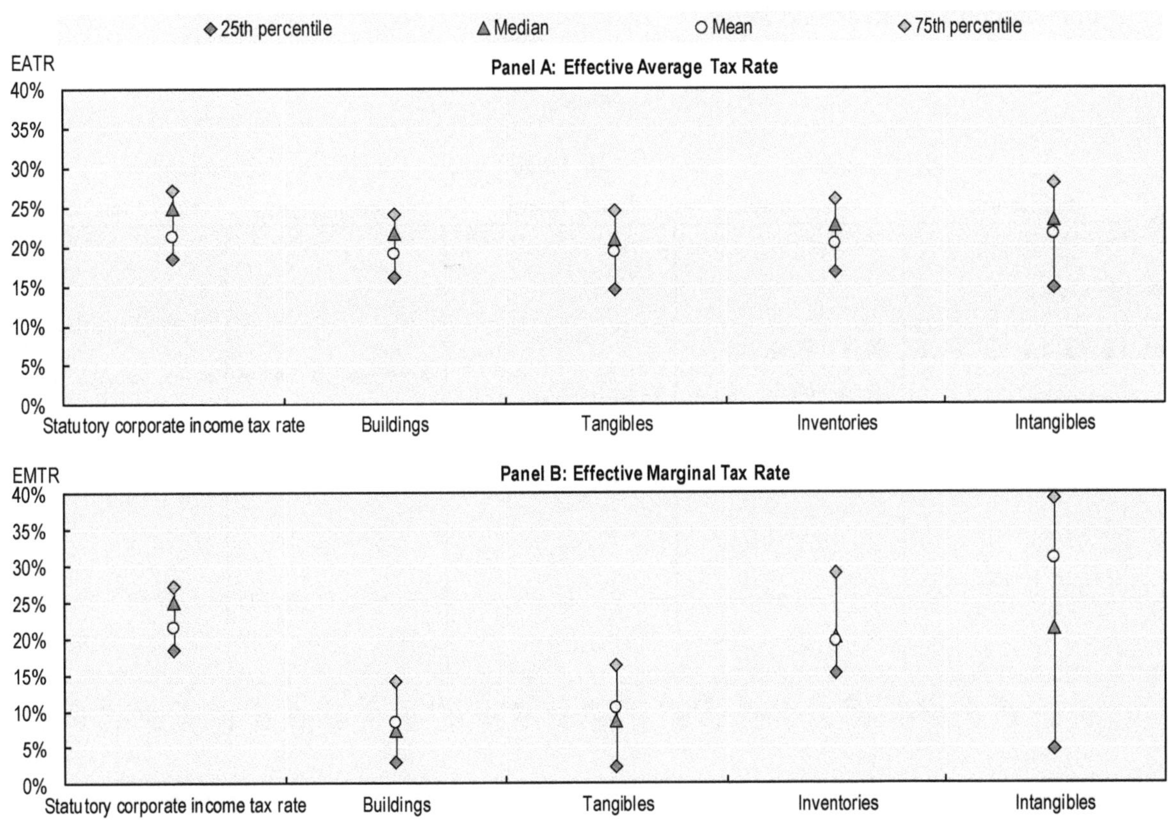

Note: The values of EMTRs and EATRs are calculated assuming a fixed inflation rate at 1% and fixed real interest rate at 3% and setting the rate of return from investments at 0%. The EMTR is computed using the tax exclusive definition (Box 3.1). Additional parameters are outlined in the ETR explanatory annex accompanying Corporate Tax Statistics. https://www.oecd.org/tax/tax-policy/explanatory-annex-corporate-effective-tax-rates.pdf.

StatLink https://stat.link/e0lzfx

Comparing the four broader asset categories with the statutory CIT rate shows that the distribution of EATRs is more condensed for investments in buildings, with the middle 50% of the country distribution ranging between 16.1% and 24.1%. For investments in tangible assets, the middle 50% of jurisdictions have EATRs between around 14.5% and 24.6%. However, the mean EATR (19.4%) on investments in tangible assets is around 1.6 p.p. lower than the median (21.0%), indicating that some jurisdictions have much lower EATRs on this type of investment. For investments in the other two asset categories, the distributions are similar to the statutory tax rate.

The lower panel illustrates the EMTR distribution for each of the four broader asset categories. The following insights emerge from this graph.

- Investments in buildings and tangible assets benefit more often from accelerated tax depreciation than other investments; as a result, the EMTRs are generally lower, and the distribution is more condensed compared to the statutory CIT rate.
- Investments in buildings have EMTRs ranging between 2.9% and 14.0% in half of the covered jurisdictions.
- Investments in inventories often benefit from lower EMTRs, compared to the statutory tax rate, although to a lesser extent than the first two asset categories.
- The tax treatment of investments in acquired software is subject to more variation across jurisdictions, which is reflected in the vertical line that stretches out more than the others, ranging from around 4.7% to around 39.1%.

Figure 3.6. Changing distribution of EATRs by assets, 2017-2022

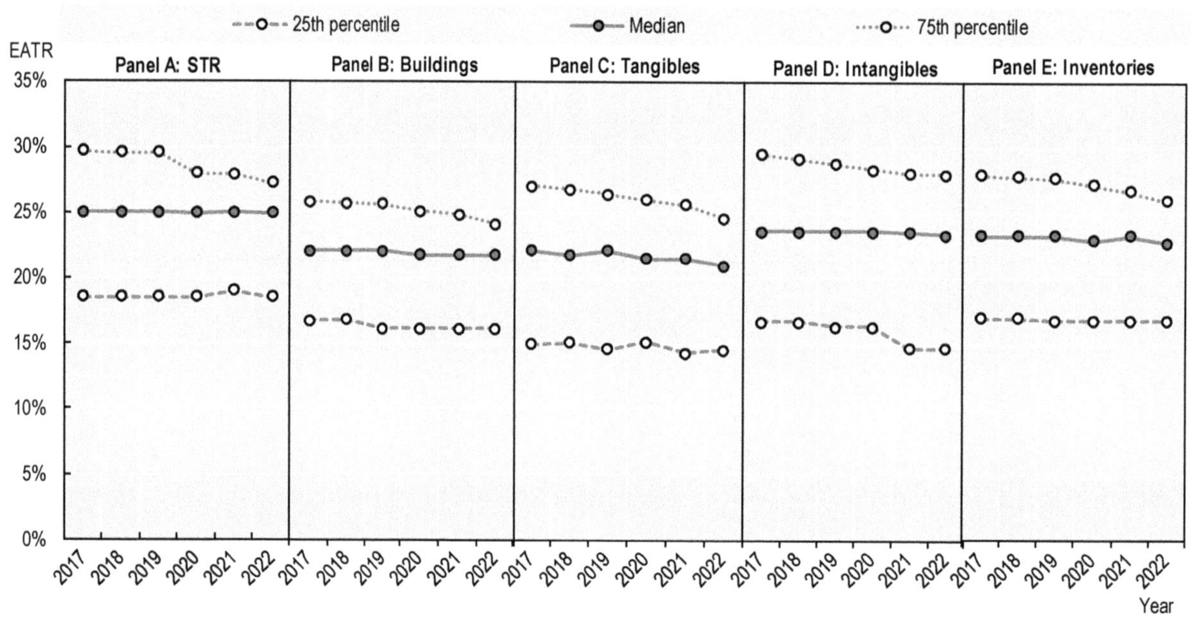

Note: The values of the EATRs are calculated assuming a fixed inflation rate at 1% and fixed real interest rate at 3% and setting the rate of return from investments at 0%. Additional parameters are outlined in the ETR explanatory annex accompanying Corporate Tax Statistics. https://www.oecd.org/tax/tax-policy/explanatory-annex-corporate-effective-tax-rates.pdf.

StatLink https://stat.link/2f57yz

When comparing Figure 3.2 to Figure 3.6, it appears that the downward trend in EATRs between 2017 and 2018 did not occur consistently throughout all asset groups and their respective distributions. While the composite EATR shows a decline in the 25th percentile between 2017 and 2018, the 25th percentile of the EATRs for buildings and tangible assets between 2017 and 2018 (Panels B and C) increased during those years. Panel D shows that between 2017 and 2018, the top of the EATR distribution fell sharply between 2017 and 2018 due to certain tax reforms in countries that had on average high EATR in the previous year. By contrast, between 2020 and 2021 the drop in EATRs for intangibles was felt more strongly in jurisdictions at the lower end of the distribution. The evolution of the median in each panel indicates that between 2017-2021, the downward trend in STRs was more pronounced than that observed for each asset specific EATR (except for inventories which follow an almost identical trend as that of STRs throughout).

Comparing median EMTRs over time, tangible assets and buildings face significantly lower EMTRs than the rest of asset categories. Figure 3.7 shows the distribution of the EMTRs disaggregated by asset types and over time. The dispersion of EMTRs is particularly marked for acquired intangibles (Panel D). This reflects important differences in the fiscal depreciation provisions applicable to acquired software between jurisdictions. Several jurisdictions in the database offer very stringent depreciation rules for acquired software. In some cases, it is non depreciable, which drives the EMTR of this asset category above the STR. Notably, the dispersion of EMTRs for tangible assets has tended to decrease over time.

Figure 3.7. Changing distribution of EMTRs by assets, 2017-2022

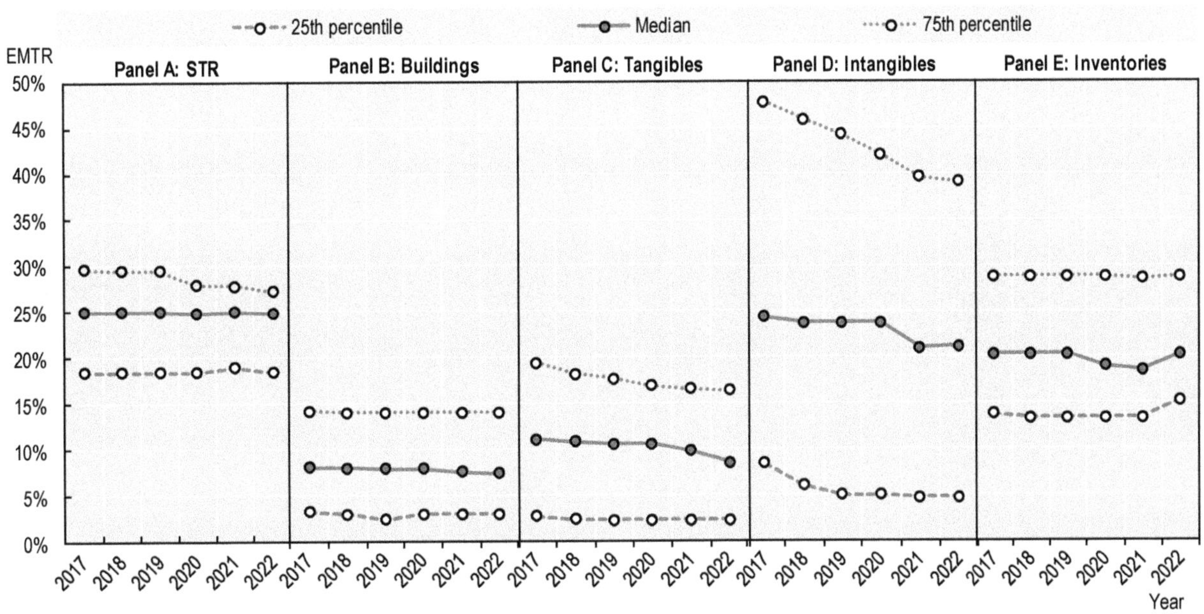

Note: The values of EMTRs are calculated assuming a fixed inflation rate at 1% and fixed real interest rate at 3% and setting the rate of return from investments at 0%. The EMTR is computed using the tax exclusive definition (Box 3.1). Additional parameters are outlined in the ETR explanatory annex accompanying Corporate Tax Statistics. https://www.oecd.org/tax/tax-policy/explanatory-annex-corporate-effective-tax-rates.pdf.

StatLink https://stat.link/wl14m9

When comparing the distribution of disaggregated EMTRs with that of EATRs, the former - as depicted by Figure 3.7 - exhibits more heterogeneity both within and between asset categories. The figure shows that during the years of coverage, the EMTR applicable to investments in buildings and tangible assets as well as the EMTR applicable to inventories are consistently lower than the STR. The EMTR for buildings and tangible assets is lower than 5% throughout the period 2017-2022 while the median STR remains above 20%. This contrast reflects that baseline CIT systems tend to provide generous fiscal depreciation for these asset types, thereby significantly reducing the cost of capital (a key element in the derivation of the EMTR) and reducing the effective tax burden on investments at the intensive margin.

Changes in the distribution of EMTR by asset type highlight the effects of certain tax reforms. Whereas Figure 3.4 shows a drop in EMTRs between 2020 and 2021, the equivalent disaggregated figure informs that this drop was neither consistent between asset groups nor within the respective distributions of asset groups. Panel C shows that an important part of the drop was driven by the relief in tax burden for marginal investments in tangible assets – particularly for jurisdictions at the top end of the distribution such as Denmark and Germany where the EMTR for tangible assets dropped by 6.4 and 11.6 p.p., respectively. During those two years, the 75th and 25th percentiles as well as the median for EMTRs applicable to inventories and buildings remained about constant. By contrast, the 25th percentile from Panel D increased at that time.

References

BEA (2003), *Fixed Assets and Consumer Durable Goods in the United States, 1925-97 | U.S. Bureau of Economic Analysis (BEA)*, https://www.bea.gov/node/24441 (accessed on 18 February 2023). [4]

Devereux, M. and R. Griffith (2003), "Evaluating tax policy for location decisions", *International Tax and Public Finance*, Vol. 10/2, pp. 107-126, https://doi.org/10.1023/A:1023364421914. [3]

Devereux, M. and R. Griffith (1998), "The taxation of discrete investment choices", https://www.econstor.eu/handle/10419/90851 (accessed on 18 February 2023). [2]

Hanappi (2018), "Corporate Effective Tax Rates : Model Description and Results from 36 OECD and Non-OECD Countries | OECD Taxation Working Papers | OECD iLibrary", https://www.oecd-ilibrary.org/taxation/corporate-effective-tax-rates_a07f9958-en (accessed on 18 February 2023). [1]

Notes

[1] In 2021, Belgium legislated a notional interest rate of 0.0% resulting in an ACE with no effect during 2021 and 2022.

[2] This range excludes the case of Belgium.

[3] The Kingdom of Saudi Arabia imposes a corporate income tax rate of 20% on a non-Saudi's' share of a resident company or a non-resident's income from a permanent establishment in Saudi Arabia or income of a company operating in the natural gas sector. A higher corporate income tax rate is imposed as well on companies operating in the oil sector (i.e., 50% or higher). The Kingdom of Saudi Arabia also levies the Zakat on companies, which is an example of a tax on both income and equity. The Zakat is levied at 2.5% on a Saudi's share of a resident company (also applies to citizens of Gulf Cooperation Council countries with an established business in the Kingdom of Saudi Arabia), but since it is imposed on income and equity, it yields a higher rate in effective terms. The Saudi government considers the corporate Zakat as an equivalent to corporate income tax, levied on a different basis. It is also considered a covered tax for the purposes of the GloBE rules in the Pillar 2 Blueprint Report (OECD, 2020). For the calculation of the forward-looking ETRs, three different groups of taxpayers are considered: (i) foreign companies as well as domestic and foreign companies in the natural gas sector taxed at 20%, (ii) domestic and foreign companies in the hydrocarbon sector taxed at 50%, (iii) other domestic companies taxed through Zakat at 2.5%. The results for these three groups of taxpayers are weighted using the respective turnover shares as weights, i.e., 18.17% for group (i), 28.72% for group (ii) and 53.11% for group (iii). The composite EATR corresponds to the combination of the unshaded and shaded blue components of each bar.

4 Tax incentives for research and development

Key insights

- Tax incentives for research and development (R&D) are increasingly used to promote business R&D with 33 out of the 38 OECD jurisdictions offering tax relief on R&D expenditures in 2021, compared to 19 in 2000.
- Most jurisdictions use a combination of direct support and tax relief to support business R&D, but the policy mix varies. Over time, there has been a shift towards a more intensive use of R&D tax incentives to deliver financial support for business R&D.
- The effective average tax rate (EATR) for R&D in 2022 was lowest in Ireland, Poland and Lithuania, providing greater tax incentives for firms to locate R&D investment in these jurisdictions.
- The cost of capital for R&D in 2022 was lowest in Portugal, Poland and France where these jurisdictions provide greater tax incentives for firms to increase their R&D investment.
- Isolating the impact of R&D tax incentives, the largest preferential tax treatment for profitable and marginal R&D investments was offered in Portugal, France and Poland in 2022.
- For profitable small and medium-sized enterprises (SMEs), implied marginal R&D tax subsidy rates were highest in Colombia, Iceland and Portugal in 2022.
- In 2022, 21 out of the 33 OECD countries that offer tax incentives offer refundable (payable) tax credits or equivalent incentives. Such provisions explicitly target SMEs and young firms compared to large enterprises in Australia, Canada and France.
- R&D tax incentives have become more generous, on average, over time. This is due to the higher uptake and increased generosity of R&D tax relief provisions. While this trend stabilised between 2013 and 2019, an increase is again observed from 2020 and maintained through to 2022.

Incentivising investment in R&D by businesses ranks high on the innovation policy agenda of many jurisdictions. R&D tax incentives have become a widely used policy tool to promote business R&D over recent decades. Several jurisdictions offer them in addition to direct forms of support such as R&D grants or government purchases of R&D services. R&D tax incentives can provide relief to R&D expenditures, such as the wages of R&D staff and/or to the income derived from R&D activities, such as patent income. The indicators referred to in this section relate to expenditure-based R&D tax incentives. An overview of income-based tax incentives is available in the section on Intellectual Property regimes. The significant variation in the design of expenditure-based R&D tax relief provisions across jurisdictions and over time affects the implied generosity of R&D tax incentives.

Indicators of R&D tax incentives

The Corporate Tax Statistics database incorporates two sets of R&D tax incentives indicators that offer a complementary view of the extent of R&D tax support provided through expenditure-based R&D tax incentives.

The first set of indicators reflects the cost of expenditure-based tax incentives to the government:

- Government tax relief for business R&D (GTARD) includes estimates of foregone revenue (and refundable amounts) from national and subnational incentives, where applicable and relevant data are available. This indicator is complemented with figures on direct funding of business R&D to provide a more complete picture of total government support to business R&D investment.
- Both indicators, compiled by the OECD Directorate for Science, Technology and Innovation, are available for 49 jurisdictions – OECD jurisdictions and 11 partner economies – for the period 2000-20.

The second set of indicators are synthetic tax policy indicators that capture the effect of expenditure-based R&D tax incentives on firms' investment costs (see Box 4.1):

- The EATR for R&D measures the impact of taxation on R&D investments that earn an economic profit.
- The user cost of capital for R&D measures the return that a firm needs to realise on an R&D investment before tax to offset all costs and taxes that arise from the investment, making zero economic profit.
- Implied marginal tax subsidy rates for R&D, calculated as 1 minus the B-Index, reflect the design and implied generosity of R&D tax incentives to firms for an extra unit of R&D outlay. The B-Index captures the extent to which different tax systems reduce the effective cost of R&D.

The second set of indicators are available for 48 countries, including OECD jurisdictions and ten partner economies. Indicators of the user cost of capital and the EATR are available for 2019-2022 and refer to large businesses who are able to fully utilise their tax benefits. Large companies account for the bulk of the R&D in most OECD countries (OECD, 2023[1]; Dernis et al., 2019[2]). The EATR and user cost for R&D are produced by the OECD Centre for Tax Policy and Administration and the OECD Directorate for Science, Technology and Innovation. The B-Index, compiled by the OECD Directorate for Science, Technology and Innovation, covers a wider group of firm scenarios (SMEs; large firms; profit and loss-making) over the 2000-2022 time period.

The indicators of ETRs and cost of capital for R&D in this section extend the corporate ETRs shown in the previous section to include internally generated R&D assets, i.e., those that are the result of a firms' own R&D.[1]

Government support for business R&D

Indicators of government tax relief for business R&D combined with data on direct R&D funding provide a more complete picture of governments' efforts to support business expenditure on R&D (BERD). Together, these indicators facilitate the cross-jurisdiction comparison of the policy mix provided by governments to support R&D and the monitoring of any changes over time.

Figure 4.1. Direct government funding and tax support for business R&D (BERD), 2020

As a percentage of gross domestic product (GDP)

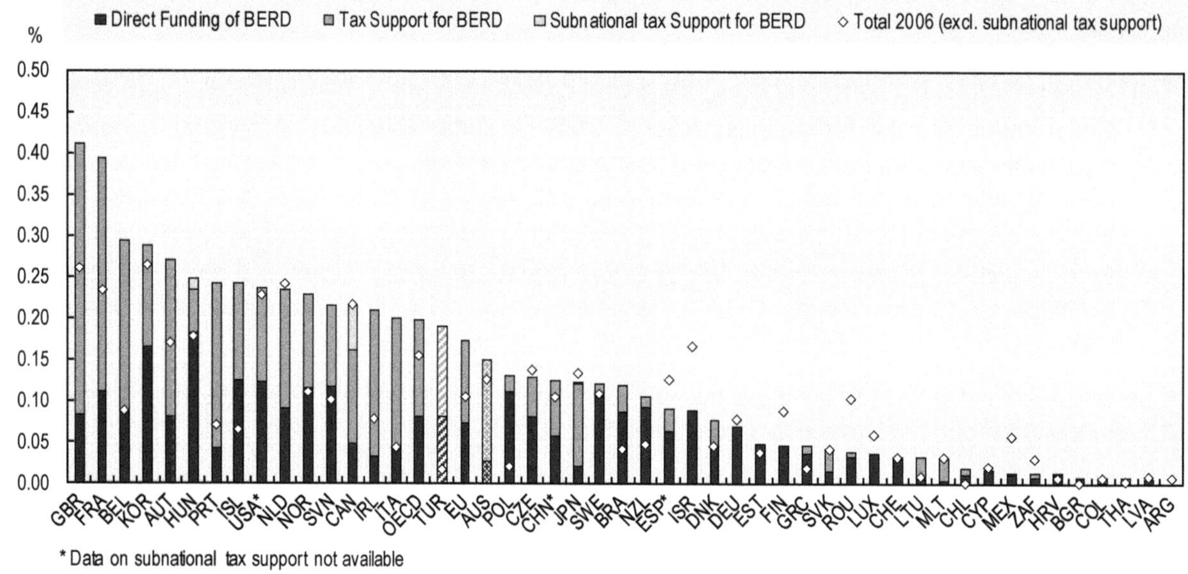

Data and notes: https://oe.cd/rdtax. Time series data available for 2000-20.
Source: OECD (2023), R&D Tax Incentive Database, http://oe.cd/rdtax, April 2023, (accessed in September 2023).

StatLink https://stat.link/7tcdam

Between 2006 and 2020, total government support (direct and national tax support) for business R&D expenditure as a percentage of GDP increased in 31 out of 46 jurisdictions for which relevant data are available. The United Kingdom, France and Austria provided the largest levels of support in 2020. Subnational R&D tax incentives accounted for 25% of total tax support in Canada in 2020, playing a comparatively smaller role in Hungary and Japan (nearly 5% and 1% of total tax support, respectively).

Most jurisdictions integrate both direct and indirect forms of R&D support in their policy mix, but to different degrees. In 2020, 16 OECD jurisdictions offered more than 50% of government support for business R&D through the tax system, and this percentage reached 75% or more in seven OECD jurisdictions: Australia, Colombia, Ireland, Italy, Japan, Lithuania and Portugal. Seven OECD jurisdictions relied solely on direct support in 2020. These are Estonia, Finland, Germany, Israel, Latvia, Luxembourg and Switzerland.

Combining time-series estimates of GTARD and direct funding helps illustrate variations in governments' policy mix over time. In recent years, many jurisdictions have granted a more prominent role to R&D tax incentives. Compared to 2006, the share of tax support in total government support in 2020 increased in 27 out of 36 OECD jurisdictions for which data are available. This implies a general shift towards less discretionary forms of support for business R&D, with some exceptions, e.g., Canada and Hungary increased their reliance on direct support.

Measuring the preferential tax treatment for R&D

R&D tax incentives exhibit very heterogeneous design features across jurisdictions, which come on top of existing differences in standard corporate income tax systems. Indicators based on forward-looking effective tax rates are therefore useful to capture in a synthetic manner the effect of taxation on firms' R&D

investment incentives. By fixing the composition of the R&D investment, they enable comparisons of the preferential tax treatment provided for R&D investments across jurisdictions.

This database provides a toolbox for policymakers to analyse the incentives that firms face through the tax system to increase their R&D investment in a given country or to (re)locate their R&D functions, taking into account both the impact of underlying corporate taxation as well as specific R&D tax incentives. Indicators calculating the EATR and the cost of capital for R&D are useful to analyse decisions at the extensive margin (e.g., whether or where to invest in R&D) and at the intensive margin (e.g., how much to invest in R&D), respectively. These indicators focus on the incentives faced by large firms among which R&D is heavily concentrated (OECD, 2023[1]; Dernis et al., 2019[2]) and assume that firms are able to use their tax benefits in full.

Governments often introduce specific provisions to target particular firm types and to promote R&D among firms that may not be able to fully use their tax benefits. The B-Index, tightly related to the cost of capital, is another useful indicator to analyse R&D investment decisions at the intensive margin and to compare differences in the implied R&D tax subsidy rates among different firm types (SMEs and large firms) and profit scenarios (profit and loss). Box 4.1 provides an overview of the three indicators.

Box 4.1. Three complementary indicators of the generosity of R&D tax support

The cost of capital, the B-Index and the EATR are conceptually linked and rely on the same modelling of R&D tax incentives. As indicators of the cost of R&D for a marginal unit of R&D outlay, the B-Index and cost of capital are used in the economic literature to assess firms' R&D investment decisions at the intensive margin, e.g., how much to invest in R&D.

The **B-Index** offers a way of comparing the generosity of R&D tax incentives in reducing the upfront investment cost of an R&D investment while abstracting from the financing of the investment. By focussing on the tax component of the cost of capital, the B-index does not require assumptions on the depreciation rate of R&D, which is typically difficult to measure, and directly displays the variation in the tax treatment induced by R&D tax incentives.

The **cost of capital** complements and extends the B-Index indicator by accounting for additional costs and taxes relevant to the R&D investment. Since the cost of capital can in principle account for a variation in economic depreciation across assets and financing options, it also facilitates the analysis of different types of R&D projects. Finally, the cost of capital is also a stepping-stone in the calculation of the EATR.

The **EATR** complements previous indicators by capturing the effect of taxation on profitable investments. This makes the EATR the relevant indicator to assess of investment decisions at the extensive margin (where or whether to invest in R&D). Together, the three indicators offer a complementary set of indicators to assess the impact of taxation on firms' R&D investment decisions.

Source: González Cabral, Appelt and Hanappi (2021[3]).

Incentives at the extensive margin

Comparing the EATRs for R&D investments across jurisdictions gives insights into the incentives provided by the tax system for the location of profitable R&D investments (Panel A). The lowest EATRs for R&D investments carried out by large firms are observed in Ireland, Poland and Lithuania, while the highest EATRs for R&D are observed in Malta, Argentina and Costa Rica. Estimates of the EATR are typically lower for jurisdictions with lower STRs or more generous provisions affecting the tax base, including both standard tax provisions and those specific to R&D investments.

To assess the preferential tax treatment for R&D investments in relation to other investments, it is useful to calculate the EATR for a comparable investment to which R&D tax incentives do not apply. Where available, R&D tax incentives decrease the effective cost of R&D and reduce firms' EATRs, as shown in Panel A by the fact that the diamonds lie lower than the circles. The extent of the reduction, shown in Panel B, is explained by the generosity of the R&D tax incentives in each jurisdiction, which is closely linked to the design of these provisions. This figure includes only the impact of tax provisions in supporting R&D: modest reductions, as in Sweden or the United States, may reflect a higher reliance on direct forms of government support for R&D.

By taking the difference between the two EATRs, it is possible to gauge the preferential tax treatment offered to R&D in a given jurisdiction, in isolation from baseline tax provisions available to all types of investments. From a within country perspective, the preferential tax treatment for R&D investments is greatest in France followed, by Poland and Portugal. The absence of bars, as in Costa Rica or Luxembourg, indicates that no preferential tax treatment for R&D is available in the jurisdiction relative to other investment types.

Figure 4.2. The effective average tax rate for R&D, 2022

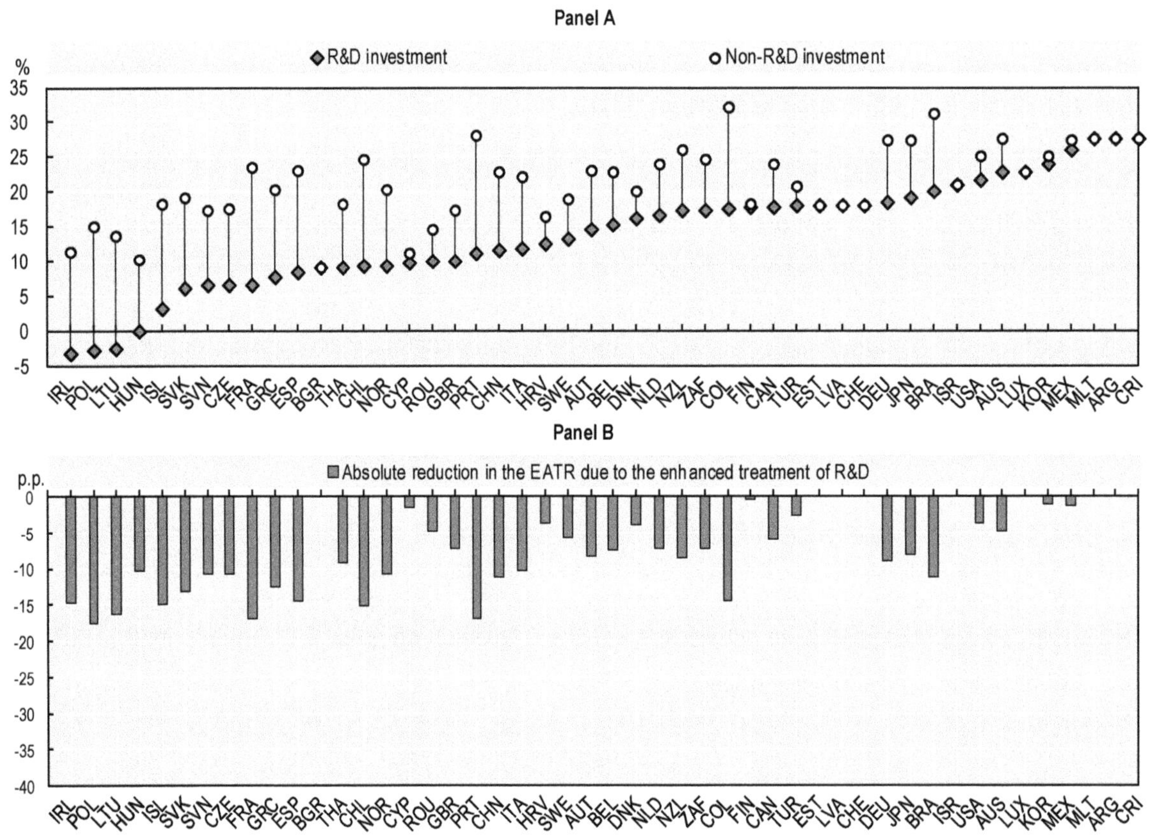

Note: Results refer to a macroeconomic scenario 3% real interest rate and 1% inflation and refer to an investment financed by retained earnings including the effect of allowances for corporate equity where available. In the non-R&D case, the EATRs lie close to the statutory tax rate (STR) due to the large current component in the R&D investment (see Box 4.1), except when an allowance for corporate equity is available.

StatLink https://stat.link/4vxni7

Figure 4.3. Changing distribution of the average EATR for R&D, 2019-2022

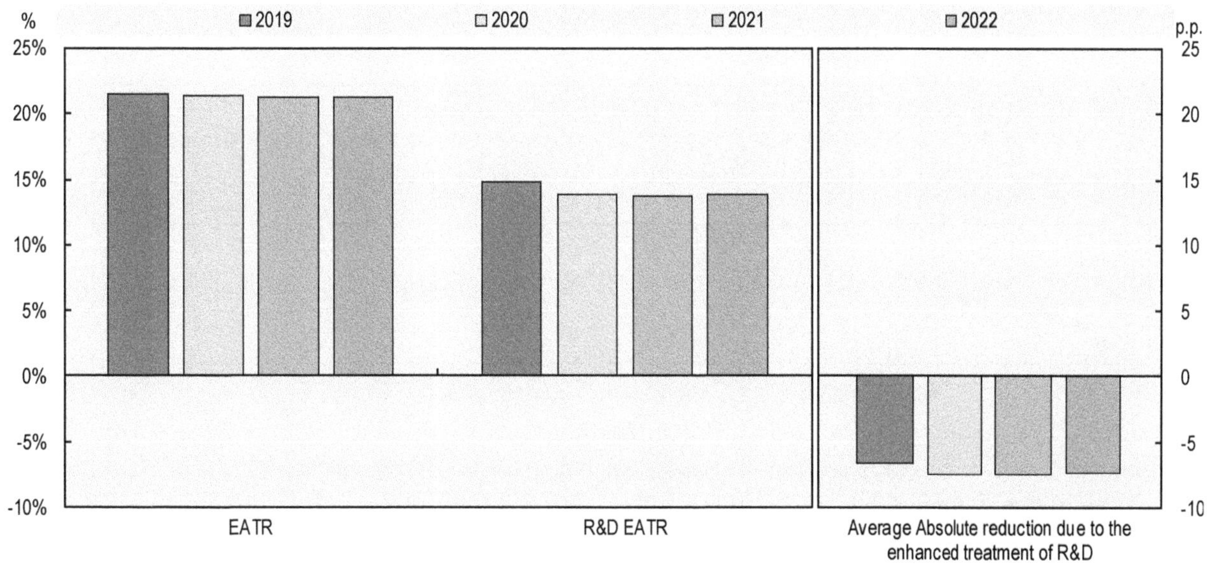

StatLink https://stat.link/2t9cyn

The EATR for R&D has modestly declined over time and while preferential tax treatment has increased compared to 2019, recent years show signs of stabilisation. Figure 4.3 displays average changes to the EATR over time. Consistent with the trends outlined in the baseline effective tax rate (ETR) (Section 3), the EATR in the absence of R&D tax incentives have tended to modestly decline over the period covered. A similar but more substantial trend is observable for the EATR once R&D tax incentives are included. The EATR for R&D declined from an average of 14.9% in 2019 to 13.9% in 2020 and to 13.9% in 2022. Changes over time in the EATR for R&D are due to first time introductions (Germany and Denmark in 2020, Finland 2021 or Cyprus in 2022) or changes to the generosity of R&D tax incentives (the Slovak Republic in 2020 and 2022, Italy in 2021 or Poland in 2022). In 2022, R&D tax incentives reduce the average EATR by 34.7%, from 21.5% to 13.9%. Over time, preferential tax treatment has increased between 2019 and 2020 and remained relatively stable between 2020 and 2022. The increase in 2020 is linked to COVID recovery measures, some of which have been maintained over time.

Incentives at the intensive margin

Once established in a given location, firms decide upon the level of investment with reference to tax provisions that affect the intensive margin. The cost of capital for R&D is one relevant indicator of tax incentives at the intensive margin. Across the jurisdictions considered Portugal, Poland and France are the jurisdictions providing greater incentives through the tax system to increase the volume of R&D. Among jurisdictions offering R&D tax support, estimates of the cost of capital for R&D are highest in Argentina, Costa Rica and Luxembourg. Estimates of the cost of capital for R&D capture both the variability in standard tax provisions and those specific to R&D investments. R&D tax incentives reduce the cost of capital, with the extent of the reduction being affected by the generosity of R&D tax incentives. The absolute difference between the cost of capital for an R&D investment and a comparable non-R&D investment provides a within-country indication of the magnitude of R&D tax relief to marginal R&D investments, net of the standard tax treatment available to all investments. This allows the preferential tax treatment for R&D to be isolated. The largest reductions in the cost of capital for R&D investments are observed in Portugal, France and Colombia, which are among the jurisdictions with the lowest cost of capital estimates.

Figure 4.4. The cost of capital for R&D, 2022

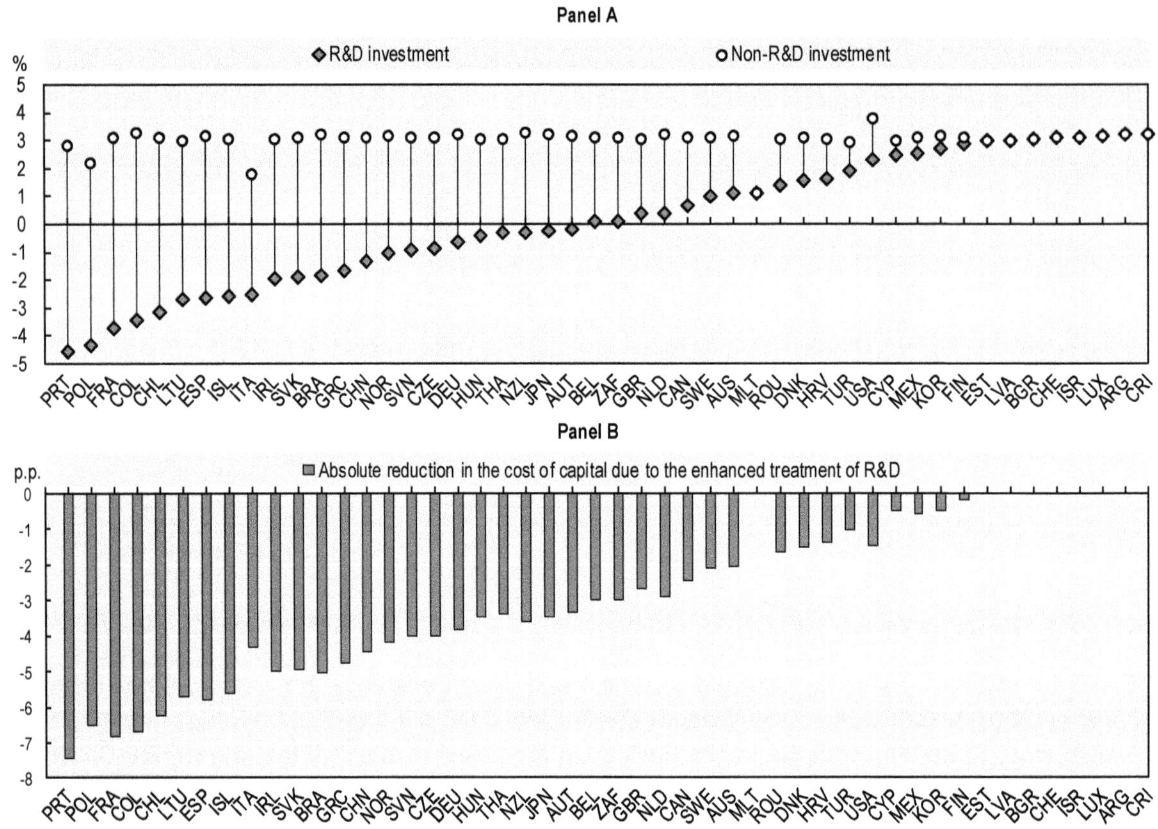

Note: Results refer to a macroeconomic scenario incorporating a 3% real interest rate and a 1% inflation rate and refer to an investment financed by retained earnings including the effect of allowances for corporate equity where available. In the non-R&D case, the cost of capital lies close to the real interest rate due to the large current component in the R&D investment (see Box 4.1), except when an allowance for corporate equity is available.

StatLink https://stat.link/k4z12o

Tax incentives significantly reduce the cost of capital for R&D and while preferential tax treatment has increased since 2019, recent years show a more stable trend. Figure 4.5 compares the evolution of the cost of R&D capital during the period 2019-2022. Similar to the EATR, the cost of capital is affected by changes in the availability of R&D tax incentives and their design. The cost of R&D capital showed a significant decline from an average of 0.4% in 2019 to 0.1% in 2020 and displayed a small increase to 0.14% in 2022. Since 2020, the implied tax subsidies have remained relatively stable, only dropping slightly in 2022. Tax incentives reduced the cost of R&D capital by 97% in 2021 and by 95% in 2022.

The heterogeneity of implied R&D tax subsidy rates

R&D tax benefits may vary with business characteristics such as firm size and profitability. Implied marginal tax subsidy rates for R&D, based on the B-Index indicator (1-B-Index), provide a synthetic indicator of the expected generosity of the tax system towards an extra unit of a firm's R&D investment (Figure 4.6). The more generous the R&D tax incentive is, the greater the value of the implied tax subsidy. This indicator shows differences in tax benefits between large and SMEs and firms in profit and loss-making positions. In jurisdictions, such as Australia or Canada, that offer enhanced tax relief provisions for SMEs that are not available to large firms, the indicator shows the difference in the implied subsidies offered to each firm type.

Figure 4.5. Changing distribution of the average cost of R&D capital, 2019-2022

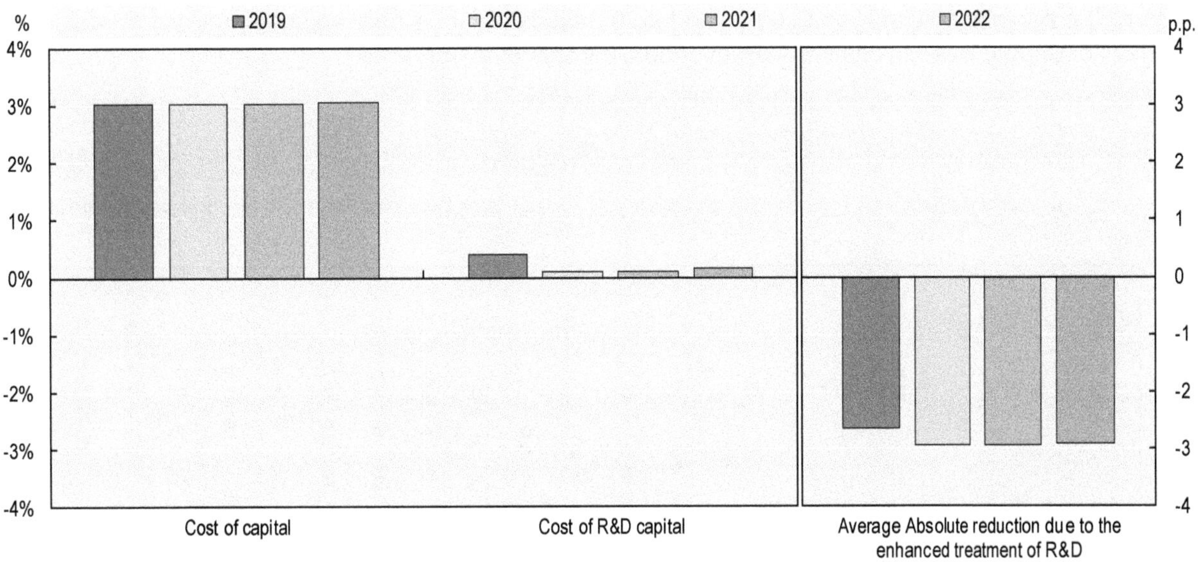

StatLink https://stat.link/ahq4ue

Figure 4.6. Implied marginal tax subsidy rates on business R&D expenditures, 2022

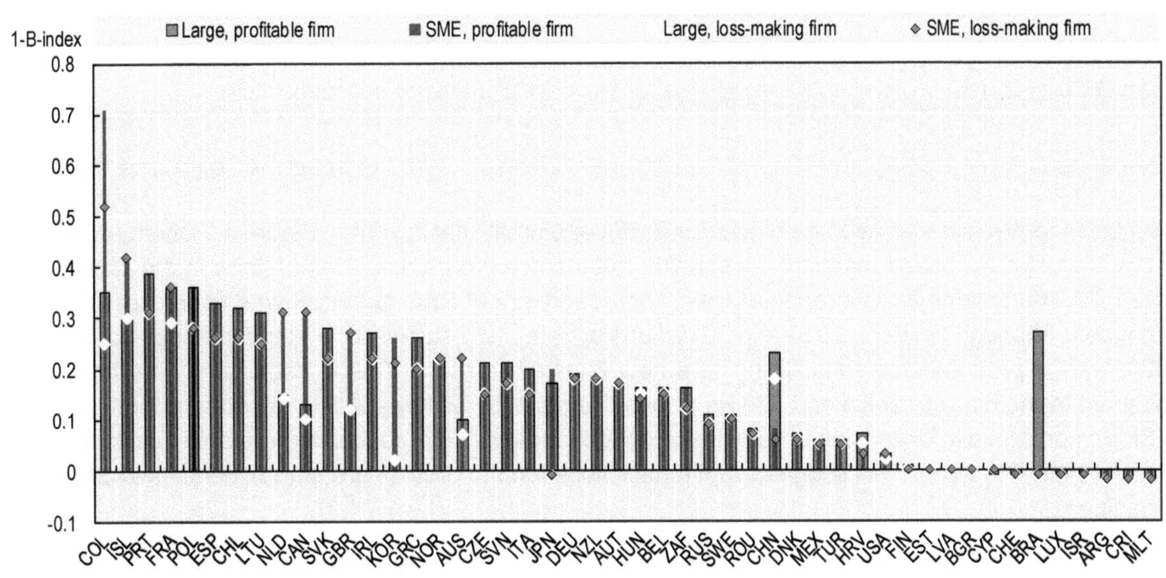

Note: Data and notes: https://oe.cd/ds/rdtax. Modelling assumes a nominal interest rate of 10%.
Source: OECD (2023), R&D Tax Incentive Database, http://oe.cd/rdtax, April 2023, (accessed in September 2023).

StatLink https://stat.link/9e8xlp

Refunds and carry-over provisions are common means of promoting R&D in firms that would not otherwise be able to utilise the support provided by the tax system. This may arise when firms do not have sufficient tax liability to offset earned deductions or do not draw a profit. Implied marginal subsidy rates are calculated under two scenarios: profitable firms (which are able to fully utilise the tax support available to them) and loss-making firms (which may not be able to fully utilise the tax support available to them) to reflect the varying impact of these provisions. Refundability provisions such as those available in Austria and Norway align the subsidy for profitable and loss-making firms. Compared to refunds, carry-over provisions, such as those available in Spain or Portugal, imply a lower subsidy for loss-making firms compared to profitable firms as the benefits may only be used in the future. In jurisdictions where no such provisions exist, such as Brazil or Japan, loss-making firms experience a full loss of tax benefits.

Figure 4.7. Evolution of the implied marginal tax subsidy rates R&D, 2000-2022

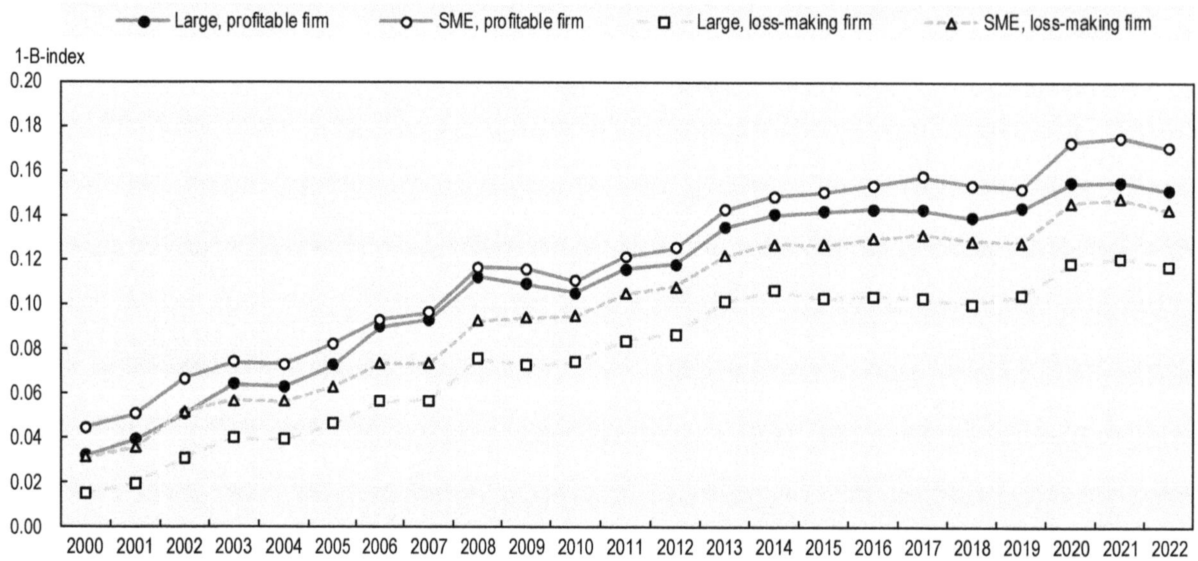

Note: Data and notes: https://oe.cd/ds/rdtax. Modelling assumes a nominal interest rate of 10%.
Source: OECD (2023), R&D Tax Incentive Database, http://oe.cd/rdtax, April 2023, (accessed in September 2023).

StatLink https://stat.link/i1aej7

R&D tax incentives are on average higher for SMEs and profit-making firms. Figure 4.7 offers an overview of the evolution of implied marginal tax subsidy rates across four categories of firms in the period 2000-2022: SMEs and large firms in profit or loss. The generosity of R&D tax incentives rises over time for all firm types. Although between 2013 and 2019 subsidy rates had stabilised, a step increase is observed in 2020, with implied subsidies stabilising at a new level since them. This is consistent with the patterns observed in the cost of capital and EATRs above. Persistently higher subsidy rates are offered over time to SMEs compared to large firms in both the profit scenarios considered; and to profitable than loss making firms for both firm types. This suggests that jurisdictions tend to provide greater tax benefits to SMEs than large firms.

The evolution of the data depicted in Figure 4.7 also reflects heterogeneity in the magnitude of year-on-year changes. The largest increase in implied marginal tax subsidy rates occurred between 2007-2008, at the time of the financial crisis, (an increase of about 2.0 p.p. throughout all four categories) and 2019-2020 (around 1.6 p.p.), at the time of the COVID pandemic.

References

Dernis, H. et al. (2019), “World Corporate Top R&D investors: Shaping the Future of Technologies and of AI. A joint JRC and OECD report.”, *Publications Office of the European Union*, https://doi.org/10.2760/16575. [2]

González Cabral, A., S. Appelt and T. Hanappi (2021), “Corporate effective tax rates for R&D: The case of expenditure-based R&D tax incentives”, https://www.oecd-ilibrary.org/taxation/corporate-effective-tax-rates-for-r-d_ff9a104f-en (accessed on 18 February 2023). [3]

OECD (2023), *OECD Main Science and Technology Indicators database*, http://www.oecd.org/sti/msti.htm (accessed on 1 September 2023). [1]

OECD (2023), *R&D Tax Incentive Database*, http://oe.cd/rdtax (accessed on 1 September 2023). [4]

Note

[1] The OECD methodology to compute effective average tax rates for R&D is described in detail in González Cabral, Appelt and Hanappi (2021[3]) and to compute the B-Index is described in OECD (2023[4]). These indicators also feature in the OECD R&D Tax Incentive database compiled by the OECD Directorate for Science, Technology and Innovation.

5 Country-by-country reporting statistics

Key insights

- The 2023 edition of *Corporate Tax Statistics* contains a further two years of anonymised and aggregated country-by-country reporting (CbCR) statistics covering fiscal years (FY) 2019 and 2020.
- Fifty-two jurisdictions out of a potential ninety-three submitted CbCR statistics to the OECD detailing the financial and business activities of almost 7 000 multinational enterprises (MNEs).
- Data for FY2019 and 2020 continues to show a misalignment between the location where profits are reported and the location where economic activities occur. Revenues and profits per employee tend to be higher in investment hubs. For example, the data show that the median value of revenues per employee in investment hubs is USD 1 630 000 as compared to just USD 290 000 for all other jurisdictions.
- The data includes a jurisdiction-by-jurisdiction breakdown of low-taxed profit of MNEs (defined as profit taxed at an effective tax rate below 15%) headquartered in some jurisdictions. This data highlights the presence of low-taxed profit in low-tax and high-tax jurisdictions alike, with more than half of the low-taxed profit in the new data located in jurisdictions with average ETRs above 15%.
- In FY 2019 and 2020 there is a large decrease in overall total profits of the MNEs covered which can be seen as a direct symptom of the COVID-19 pandemic.
- The composition of business activity differs across jurisdiction groups. The most predominant activity in investment hubs is "holding shares" which also includes other equity instruments.

Country-by-country reporting was implemented as part of Action 13 of the OECD/G20 BEPS Project to support jurisdictions in combating base erosion and profit shifting (BEPS). Under BEPS Action 13, all large MNEs are required to prepare a country-by-country (CbC) report with aggregate data on the global allocation of income, profit, taxes paid and economic activity among tax jurisdictions in which it operates. This CbC report is shared with tax administrations in these jurisdictions, for use in high level transfer pricing and BEPS risk assessments.

While the main purpose of country-by-country reports is to support tax administrations in the high-level detection and assessment of transfer pricing and other BEPS-related risks, data collected from CbCRs can also play a role in supporting the economic and statistical analysis of BEPS activity and of multinational enterprises in general. Under Action 11 of the BEPS Project (OECD, 2015[1]), acknowledging the need for additional sources of data on MNEs, jurisdictions agreed to regularly publish anonymised and aggregated CbCR statistics to support the ongoing economic and statistical analysis of MNEs and BEPS. This section outlines progress on the implementation of Action 13, as well as the country-by-country reporting statistics published by the OECD under Action 11.

Action 13 implementation

BEPS Action 13 is part of the transparency pillar of the OECD/G20 BEPS project, supporting jurisdictions in combating BEPS. In many cases, jurisdictions already have rules in place to deal with BEPS risks posed by MNE groups but may not previously have had access to information to identify cases where these risks arise. BEPS Action 13 helps to address this by providing new information for use by tax administrations in high-level transfer pricing risk assessment and the assessment of other BEPS-related risks.

For the fiscal year 2020, 93 jurisdictions required mandatory filing of Country-by-Country Reports for 2020. To date, more than 100 jurisdictions have laws in place introducing a reporting obligation in relation to CbCRs (Figure 5.1).

Feedback from tax administrations indicates that they are using CbCRs to combat BEPS, in combination with other tools: (i) to help identify MNE groups for possible audit, (ii) to help identify MNE groups that do not need to be audited (de-selection), and (iii) to help plan audits or other enquiries. The specific approaches adopted vary depending upon each tax administration's general approach to risk assessment. Two important points to note on the role of CbCRs include:

- **CbCRs may only be used in a high-level risk assessment of an MNE.** CbCRs may not be used as evidence that BEPS exists or as a substitute for substantive enquiries and should be used alongside other information available to tax administrations. It is unlikely that success in particular cases will be able to be attributed to CbCRs specifically.
- **There may be a significant time delay between a CbCR being filed and the outcomes of a transfer pricing audit.** CbCRs may be used for the purposes of a high-level risk assessment and in planning a tax audit, but it will only be determined whether an MNE group is in fact engaged in BEPS once further enquiries are completed, which may take a number of years.

While CbCRs are an important tool, tax administrations are using them in concert with a range of other tools in their efforts to combat BEPS. The OECD has developed several tools to support tax administrations in using CbCRs and, in particular, in undertaking multilateral activity to risk assess MNE groups. These include regular CbCR risk assessment workshops; the CbCR Tax Risk Evaluation and Assessment Tool (TREAT) for tax administrations; a Tax Risk Assessment Questionnaire (TRAQ), which is used in the International Compliance Assurance Programme (ICAP) provided by a tax administration to an MNE group with an invitation to explain key indicators of possible risk; and the CbCR Effective Risk Assessment Handbook, released in 2017.

The number of jurisdictions providing CbCR statistics has increased yearly since their introduction in 2016. Figure 5.2 shows that the total number of jurisdictions that could potentially provide CbCR statistics to the OECD increased from 58 in 2016 to 93 in 2020. This total is calculated as the number of jurisdictions that have implemented mandatory CbCR filing along with those that accepted voluntary filing in the specific year. For example, in 2016, 49 jurisdictions implemented mandatory filing while a further 9 accepted voluntary filing. The number of jurisdictions that provided CbCR statistics increased from 26 to 52 over the same period. Despite the large increase in the number of jurisdictions that could potentially submit CbCR statistics the number of jurisdictions that did not provide CbCR statistics to the OECD has only increased from 32 to 41. Many jurisdictions receive too few CbCRs to be able to provide the statistics under their confidentiality standards.

Figure 5.1. Number of jurisdictions implementing mandatory CbCR filing

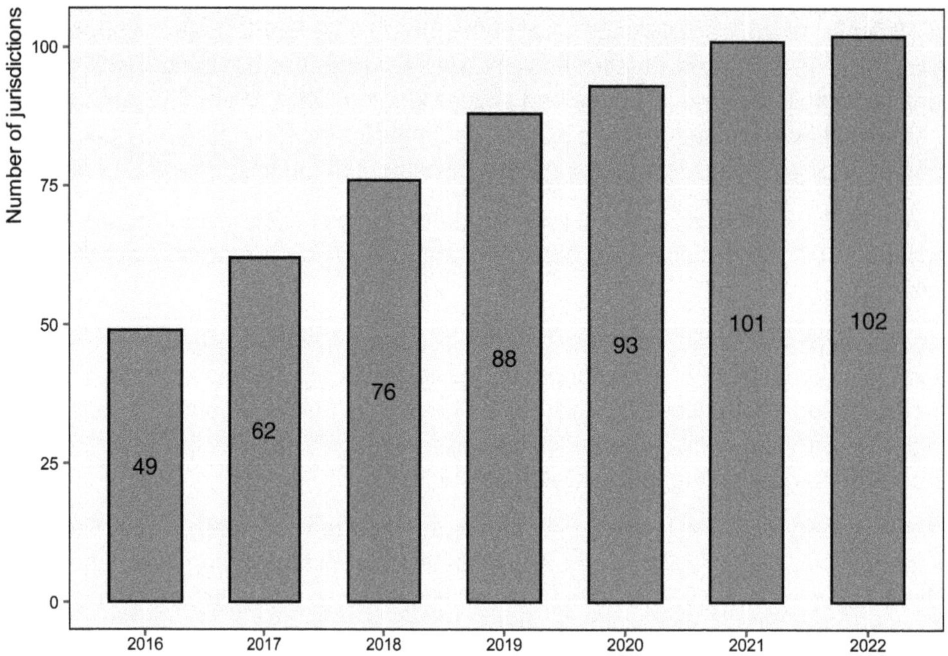

Source: Action 13 Automatic exchange portal (https://oe.cd/3Kj).

StatLink https://stat.link/plfzw8

Figure 5.2. The evolution of CbCR coverage

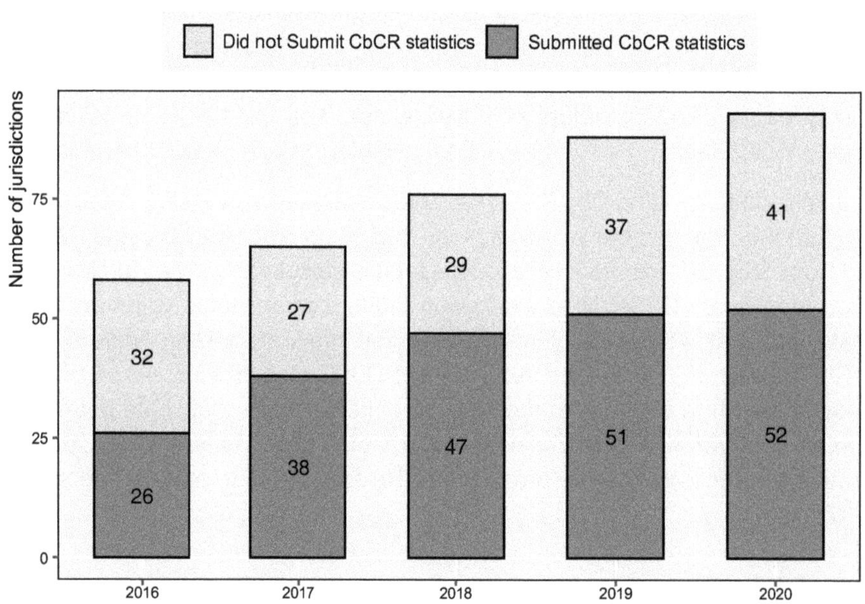

Source: Anonymised and Aggregated CbCR statistics and OECD Country-by-Country Reporting Requirements.

StatLink https://stat.link/dlqyav

General CbCR data characteristics

Jurisdictions have provided the OECD with anonymised and aggregated tabulations of the Country by Country Reporting information described below. Aggregation is performed at the sub-group level according to certain sub-group or group characteristics and reported according to these different criteria in several tables (see Box 5.1). Table 5.1 provides an overview of the tables submitted to the OECD as part of the CbCR statistics, a brief description of their content and the number of individual jurisdictions that submitted each table in 2018.

The aggregated CbCR data are subject to a number of limitations that need to be borne in mind when carrying out any economic or statistical analysis (see Box 5.2). Nonetheless, the data provide important information on MNEs and their activities relative to previously existing data sources:

- The CbCR data provide global information on MNEs' activities, with more granular information than is available in other data sources such as consolidated financial accounts.[1]
- The CbCR data include information on number of CbCRs, number of sub-groups, number of entities, total unrelated and related party revenues (and their sum, total revenues), profit or loss before income tax, income tax paid (on a cash basis), current year income tax accrued, stated capital, accumulated earnings, number of employees, tangible assets other than cash and cash equivalents, and the main business activity (or activities) of each constituent entity.
- The data ensure inclusion of all global activities of included MNEs.
- At a minimum, the data allows for the domestic and foreign activities of MNEs to be separately identified.[2] Depending on the reporting jurisdiction, it allows for an analysis of MNEs' activities in investment hubs and developing jurisdictions thanks to a detailed geographical disaggregation.
- Information is reported by jurisdiction of tax residence and not jurisdiction of incorporation.
- The CbCR data provide cross-country information on MNEs' business activities (e.g., manufacturing, intellectual property (IP) holding, sales) in different jurisdictions, allowing researchers to relate financial outcomes to these functions for the first time.

The CbCR data thus provide governments and researchers with important new information to analyse MNE behaviour, particularly in relation to tax, allowing for the construction of a more complete view of the global activities of the largest MNEs than is possible using existing sources.

The anonymised and aggregated CbCR statistics are constructed in two main steps. First, all large MNEs (i.e., with consolidated revenues of at least EUR 750 million) file CbCRs, typically with the tax administration in the jurisdiction of their ultimate parent entity (UPE). An MNE group is usually required to file its CbCR one year after the closing date of its fiscal year. Second, in each jurisdiction, tax administrations or other government bodies compile the different CbCR filings into a single dataset according to their specific confidentiality standards. This results in a single anonymised and aggregated dataset covering all the jurisdiction's MNEs subject to the filing requirement, which is shared with the OECD.

Box 5.1. MNE group structure

An **MNE group** is a collection of enterprises related through ownership or control such that the group is either required to prepare consolidated financial statements for financial reporting purposes under applicable accounting principles or would be so required if equity interests in any of the enterprises were traded on a public securities exchange.

An **entity** is any separate business unit of an MNE group that is included in the consolidated financial statements of the MNE group for financial reporting purposes.

The **UPE** directly or indirectly owns a sufficient interest in one or more other entities of the MNE group such that it is required to prepare consolidated Financial Statements.

A **sub-group** is formed by the combined entities of an MNE group operating in one tax jurisdiction.

Table 5.1. Content of anonymised and aggregated CbCR statistics

CbCR table	Content	Description
Table 1A	Aggregate totals of all variables by jurisdiction	Reports variable totals for all sub-groups, obtained by aggregating sub-group variables according to their jurisdiction of tax residence (or jurisdiction groups, depending on confidentiality). The tables include three panels aggregating all sub-groups, sub-groups with positive profits and sub-groups with negative profits.
Table 1B	Interquartile mean values of all variables by jurisdiction	Same structure as Table 1A but with interquartile mean figures based on the number of CbCR sub-groups.
Table 4	Aggregate totals of all variables by effective tax rate of MNE groups	Data is provided by effective tax rate of the MNE group and by tax jurisdiction. The level of disaggregation varies across jurisdictions, depending on confidentiality.
Table 5	Aggregate totals of all variables by effective tax rate of MNE sub-groups	Data is provided by the effective tax rate of the MNE sub-group. The level of disaggregation varies across jurisdictions, depending on confidentiality.
Table 6	Distribution points of MNE group size	Provides distribution points of MNE group size, as measured by unrelated party revenues, number of employees and tangible assets. The total size of an MNE group is determined by summing the relevant variables across all of its sub-groups.

Note: The collection of Tables 2 and 3, where the data is aggregated according to the MNEs sector and size, has been postponed. The Inclusive Framework will consider whether to expand the dataset to include these tables in future years. The effective tax rate (ETR) of the MNE group and sub-group in Tables 4 and 5 should not be directly compared to the effective tax rates mentioned in the chapter on corporate effective tax rates.

Coverage of CbCR statistics

While there are 141 members of the Inclusive Framework, only 93 have implemented mandatory reporting for the fiscal year 2020 (see above). The 2023 edition of *Corporate Tax Statistics* includes CbCR statistics on CbCRs filed in 52 jurisdictions, covering almost 7 600 MNE groups (see Table 5.2). This dataset contains a vast array of information on the global financial and economic activities of MNEs.

Anonymised and aggregated CbCR data provide an overview of where large MNE groups are headquartered. Table 5.2 shows that, across the jurisdictions that submitted data, the United States and Japan host almost 40% of the headquarters of MNEs included in the sample. The number of reported MNEs varies considerably among jurisdictions, ranging from a minimum of two in Macau, China to 1,759 in the United States. The median number of reported MNEs per jurisdiction is 64.

The number of MNEs covered in the CbCR statistics has increased over time, from 3,722 in 2016 to 7,583 in 2020. Panel A of Figure 5.3 shows the breakdown of MNE headquarters by regional grouping. There is a fairly even split of headquarter locations between the Americas, Asia & Oceania and Europe across the sample. However, Panel B of Figure 5.3 shows that in general, MNEs in Asia & Oceania comprise more business entities than in the other regional groupings.

Box 5.2. Limitations of the CbCR data and actions to improve the quality of the data

The aggregated CbCR data are subject to a number of limitations that need to be borne in mind when carrying out any economic or statistical analysis. Some limitations include that:

- Much of the data is too aggregated to allow detailed investigation of specific BEPS channels (e.g., there is no distinction between royalties and interest in related party payments, and no information on intangible assets).
- Often but not always, CbCRs are based on financial accounting data.[3] Due to differences between financial and other permitted accounting rules and tax reporting rules, CbCR data might not accurately represent how items are reported for tax purposes. Differences in accounting rules could affect the comparability of CbCR data across jurisdictions.
- There are a number of data deficiencies described in the disclaimer accompanying the data, which is available at http://www.oecd.org/tax/tax-policy/anonymised-and-aggregated-cbcr-statistics-disclaimer.pdf. In the absence of specific guidance, MNEs may have included intra-company dividends in profit figures, meaning that profit figures could be subject to double counting.
- While the inclusion of dividends in the profit figure is normal in separate financial accounting, in the context of corporate income tax analysis it can lead to biased results. For example, the tax treatment of repatriated dividends can differ across jurisdictions. As a distribution of post-tax profits, dividends are often lightly taxed or tax exempt.[4] To evaluate the potential magnitude of included dividends, some jurisdictions have carried out their own independent analyses of this question.[5]
- In the case of stateless entities, the inclusion of transparent entities such as partnerships may give rise to double counting of revenue and profit. On the other hand, the data may imply that stateless profit are untaxed, since this income is generally taxed at the level of the owner.
- Corporate income tax (CIT) exempt companies such as pension funds or university hospitals are required to file CbCRs and as such are included in aggregated statistics, unless otherwise specified. The inclusion of these companies could distort the relationship between profits and taxes.

Some of the data limitations have already been addressed through revised guidance. For example, with respect to the double-counting of dividends, the guidance on CbCR implementation was updated in November 2019 to specify that intra-company dividends should be excluded from profit figures. However, because of the time lag in the revision of instructions with jurisdictions and in reporting, it is expected to take several years before these actions lead to improvements in data quality. Other issues, e.g., the treatment of stateless entities, are the subject of ongoing discussion, including through the review of Country-by-Country Reporting (BEPS Action 13)[6] that could lead to the collection of more detailed information through CbCR reports in the future. The OECD continues to work with members of the Inclusive Framework and other stakeholders to improve the quality and consistency of the data across jurisdictions. In light of these potential improvements, it is expected that the value and importance of the dataset in providing researchers and the public with a valuable tool for better understanding the global activities of MNEs and BEPS will continue to increase over time.

In addition to the limitations mentioned above, caution needs to be exercised when attempting to draw conclusions from the data for several reasons:

- Changes and potential trends in BEPS behaviour cannot be detected with a single year of data.
- In the short term, comparability between the 2016 and the 2017 and 2018 samples is limited, e.g., because of the move from voluntary to mandatory filing and differences in fiscal year coverage.[7] In the longer term, changes to guidance will lead to changing treatment of some variables such as profits, also limiting the comparison of these variables over time.
- Even with additional years of data, a number of other events that affect the data may make it difficult to identify the effect of BEPS-related policies (e.g., COVID-19, and the United States' 2017 Tax Cuts and Jobs Act).
- Implementing BEPS measures takes time, and the effects of these measures may not become evident until a few years after implementation.

Figure 5.3. Distribution of MNEs and entities by region

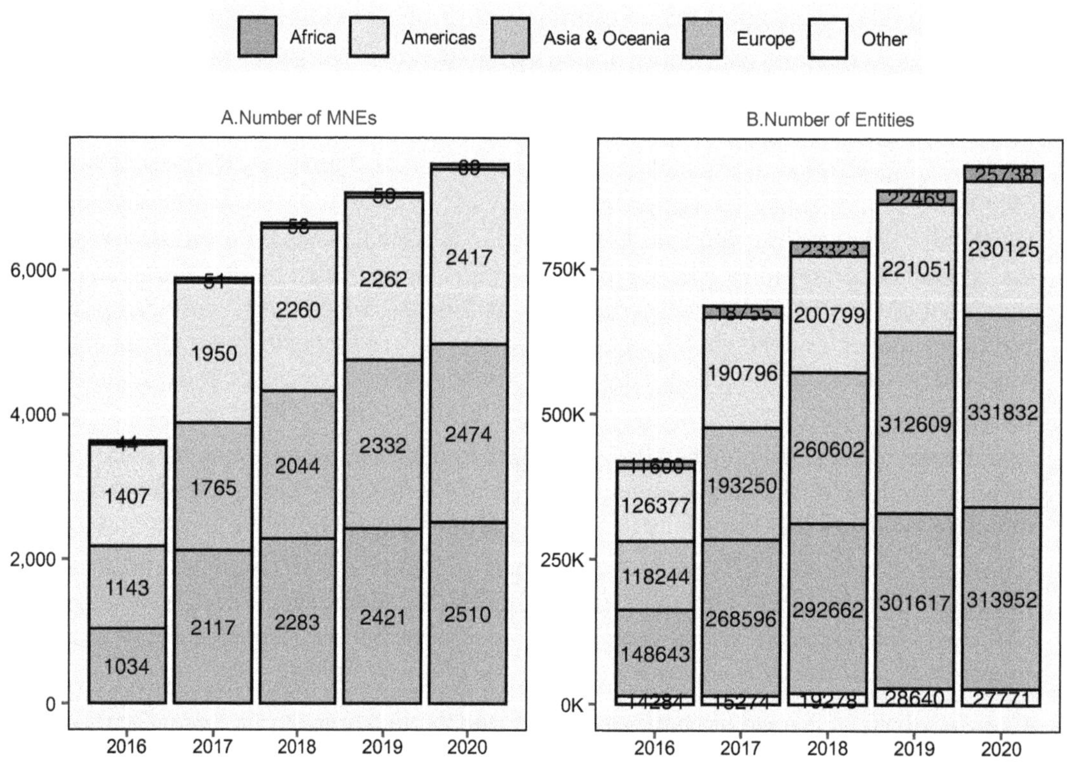

Source: Anonymised and aggregated CbCR statistics.

StatLink https://stat.link/3jql1t

Table 5.2. Sample composition and average values for key financial variables

	Reporting Jurisdiction	Level of data disaggregation	Number of CbCRs	Unrelated party revenues	Tangible assets (other than cash)	Income tax accrued	Number of employees
1	Argentina	16 individual jurisdictions	30	1 539	3 160	27	7 361
2	Australia	92 individual jurisdictions	148	4 055	3 710	117	11 240
3	Austria	Continents	100	3 851	2 576	38	12 477
4	Belgium	22 individual jurisdictions	69	4 147	2 997	77	12 175
5	Bermuda	96 individual jurisdictions	71	4 472	4 888	63	12 291
6	Brazil	33 individual jurisdictions	82	8 789	7 680	134	22 641
7	Bulgaria	4 individual jurisdictions	3	1 792	3 829	19	9 716
8	Canada	9 individual jurisdictions	230	5 664	6 085	112	14 080
9	Cayman Islands	138 individual jurisdictions	135	7 776	8 466	211	25 249
10	Chile	12 individual jurisdictions	31	3 796	3 844	56	20 707
11	China	133 individual jurisdictions	691	13 755	12 535	285	39 014
12	Czechia	All foreign jurisdictions combined					
13	Denmark	101 individual jurisdictions	73	5 044	3 505	115	16 877
14	Finland	Continents	52	5 296	1 979	65	11 323
15	France	88 individual jurisdictions	235	10 269	5 730	217	36 748
16	Germany	162 individual jurisdictions	419	8 316	5 276	113	22 961
17	Greece	68 individual jurisdictions	17	3 559	2 882	39	10 083
18	Hong Kong, China	138 individual jurisdictions	231	5 013	8 289	148	18 425
19	Hungary	All foreign jurisdictions combined	8	4 373	2 174	44	13 842
20	India	83 individual jurisdictions	144	5 129	6 608	109	32 861
21	Indonesia	71 individual jurisdictions	27	4 764	11 587	89	22 326
22	Ireland	All foreign jurisdictions combined	63	6 085	3 021	109	29 150
23	Isle Of Man	Continents	6	1 509	954	7	4 217
24	Italy	103 individual jurisdictions	143	5 163	3 087	75	12 326
25	Japan	135 individual jurisdictions	904	7 546	4 229	135	19 433
26	Korea	Continents	247	7 393	5 604	127	15 039
27	Latvia	10 individual jurisdictions	3	217	1 315	9	2 520
28	Lithuania	4 individual jurisdictions	4	1 392	1 324	12	6 806
29	Luxembourg	98 individual jurisdictions	155	3 924	2 118	20	11 324
30	Macau, China	All foreign jurisdictions combined	2	1 162	6 620	9	14 946
31	Malaysia	26 individual jurisdictions	62	4 022	13 904	88	18 548
32	Mauritius	Continents	8	4 978	2 971	26	5 080
33	Mexico	91 individual jurisdictions	64	19 798	13 653	206	32 479
34	Netherlands	5 individual jurisdictions	162	22 852	7 656	231	22 199
35	New Zealand	All foreign jurisdictions combined	23	2 915	2 384	29	6 499
36	Norway	59 individual jurisdictions	66	3 471	3 409	70	6 606
37	Panama	48 individual jurisdictions	5	3 891	4 637	12	37 823
38	Peru	13 individual jurisdictions	10	2 443	1 809	48	6 233
39	Poland	5 individual jurisdictions	28	4 791	3 459	85	16 463
40	Portugal	48 individual jurisdictions	23	3 324	1 195	25	11 893
41	Romania	146 individual jurisdictions	4	34 185	12 848	329	63 982
42	Saudi Arabia	96 individual jurisdictions	35	9 712	17 509	1 394	14 202
43	Singapore	27 individual jurisdictions	73	6 425	5 097	85	11 995
44	Slovenia	5 individual jurisdictions	6	2 303	961	17	5 341
45	South Africa	38 individual jurisdictions	58	3 613	2 838	82	32 973
46	Spain	106 individual jurisdictions	139	5 066	3 776	64	18 961
47	Sweden	Continents	117	4 097	2 004	89	14 594
48	Switzerland	139 individual jurisdictions	159	7 799	5 068	138	18 859
49	Tunisia	9 individual jurisdictions	3	2 137	2 447	28	10 873

50	Turkey	45 individual jurisdictions	57	5 263	2 333	86	17 432
51	United Kingdom	Continents	399	7 363	4 690	145	21 150
52	United States	139 individual jurisdictions	1 759	9 254	4 888	164	22 395

Note: Currency values (all values except the number of CbCRs and number of employees) are reported in millions of USD. Level of data disaggregation provided depends on data confidentiality standards applicable in each reporting jurisdiction. Average values have not been calculated for Czechia as the number of CbCRs has not been supplied for confidentiality reasons.
Source: Anonymised and Aggregated CbCR statistics.

Foreign and domestic MNEs account for significant shares of CIT revenues in several jurisdictions. For a selection of countries, Figure 5.4 reports total tax accrued based on CbCR statistics, as a fraction of the total national CIT revenues, taken from the OECD's Global Revenue Statistics Database. The figure allows an examination of the relative importance of foreign and domestic MNE contributions as covered in the 2020 data.[8]

Figure 5.5 shows the variation of MNEs contribution to total CIT revenues as compared to 2019. Twenty jurisdictions saw a net increase in the contribution of MNEs to their total CIT revenues. The percentage contribution by Greek and Mauritian MNEs increased by over 20 p.p. in 2020. On the other hand, six jurisdictions saw a decrease of more than 10 p.p. between 2019 and 2020.

MNEs operate both within their domestic jurisdiction where the UPE is located and in foreign jurisdictions where their foreign entities are located. Figure 5.6 provides detailed information about the distribution of MNE activities between domestic and foreign jurisdictions where activities operated abroad are disaggregated into regional groupings. The upward trend across most panels is associated in line with the increasing coverage in MNEs as depicted in Figure 5.3, however, the large decrease in total profits can be seen as a symptom of the COVID-19 pandemic.

Panels A-D shows the location of selected financial activities, ranging from unrelated party revenues (UPR) in panel A to assets in panel D. The distribution of panel A shows that 20 out of 31 and 36 out of 62 USD trillions in UPR were located domestically in 2016 and 2020, respectively. This entails that in the years for which data is available, the majority of the activity in question takes place domestically. This trend is identical in panels B-D as well as in panel E which depicts the distribution of employees. Panel F, which captures the distribution of entities, is an exception in this respect. The figure shows that the share of domestic entities was around one third across the years 2016 to 2020. The available data thereby suggests that when MNEs set up an entity, in most cases the entity is based in a foreign jurisdiction in comparison with the location of the UPE.

Figure 5.4. MNEs' contribution to total CIT Revenues, 2020

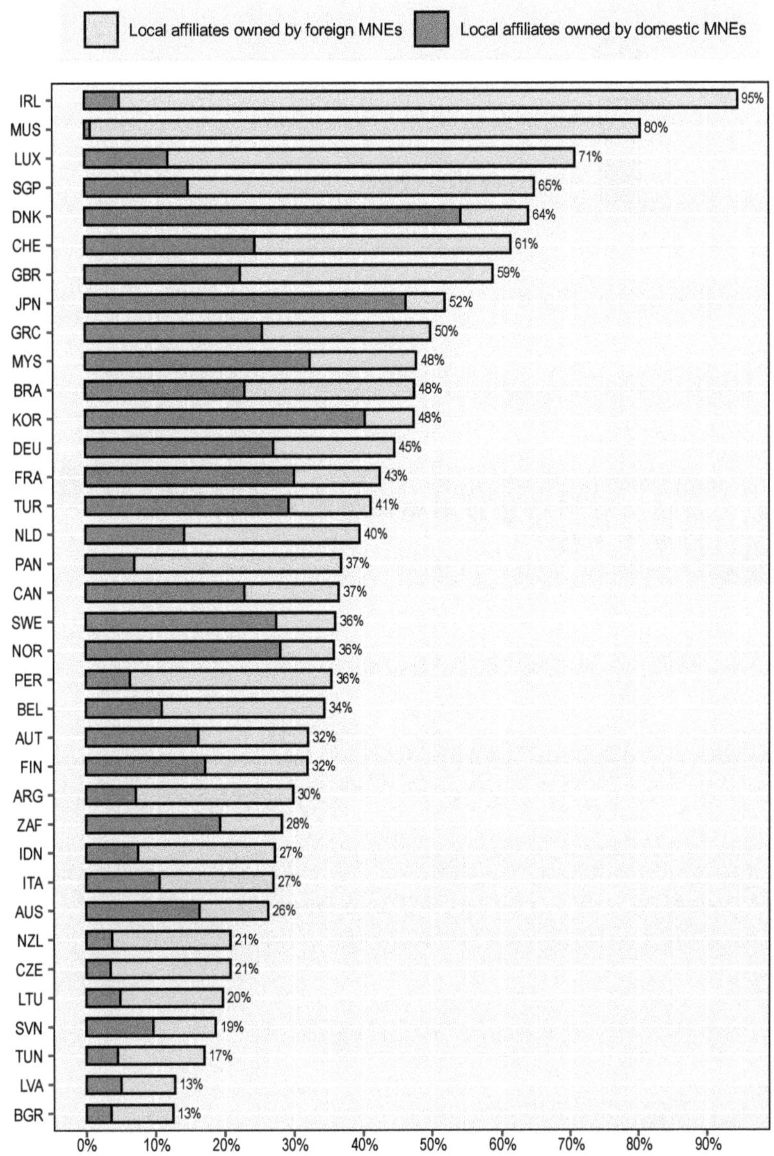

Note: The percentages above are calculated by dividing the amount of total tax accrued reported in CbCR statistics by total CIT revenues as reported in the OECD's Global Revenue Statistics Database. The figure shows total revenues of both domestic and foreign MNEs as a percentage of total CIT revenues, with jurisdictions ranked according to the total contribution of MNEs to CIT revenues. As there might be some timing differences in recording tax payments between tax accrued reported in CbCR data and CIT revenues reported in Global Revenue Statistics, percentages should be considered as indicative. Revenues from foreign MNEs are calculated as the sum of tax accrued reported in the jurisdiction by MNEs headquartered in other jurisdictions. Foreign MNEs' tax revenues should be considered as a lower bound as they can be reported exclusively where the geographical disaggregation is available at the jurisdiction level. Data for missing jurisdictions are not included because these jurisdictions are not covered in the 2020 OECD Global Revenue Statistics data. The US ratio of MNE tax revenues to total tax revenues is not presented in this chart due to a one-time transition tax imposed as part of the 2017 Tax Cuts and Jobs Act, which created a mismatch between the numerator and denominator of this ratio. MNEs generally report this transition tax as part of income taxes accrued and income taxes paid on the CbCR. However, the US Bureau of Economic Analysis does not classify this transition tax as CIT revenue (https://www.bea.gov/help/faq/1293). Therefore, the ratio of income tax accrued in CbCR data to US CIT revenues would be significantly upward biased and not indicative of the amount of CIT revenue contributed by MNEs in 2020. This mismatch is likely to persist for a number of years as taxpayers can elect to pay the tax over several years.

Source: 2020 Anonymised and Aggregated CbCR statistics and the OECD Global Revenue Statistics Database.

StatLink https://stat.link/beav2d

Figure 5.5. 2020 MNEs' contribution to total CIT Revenues compared to 2019

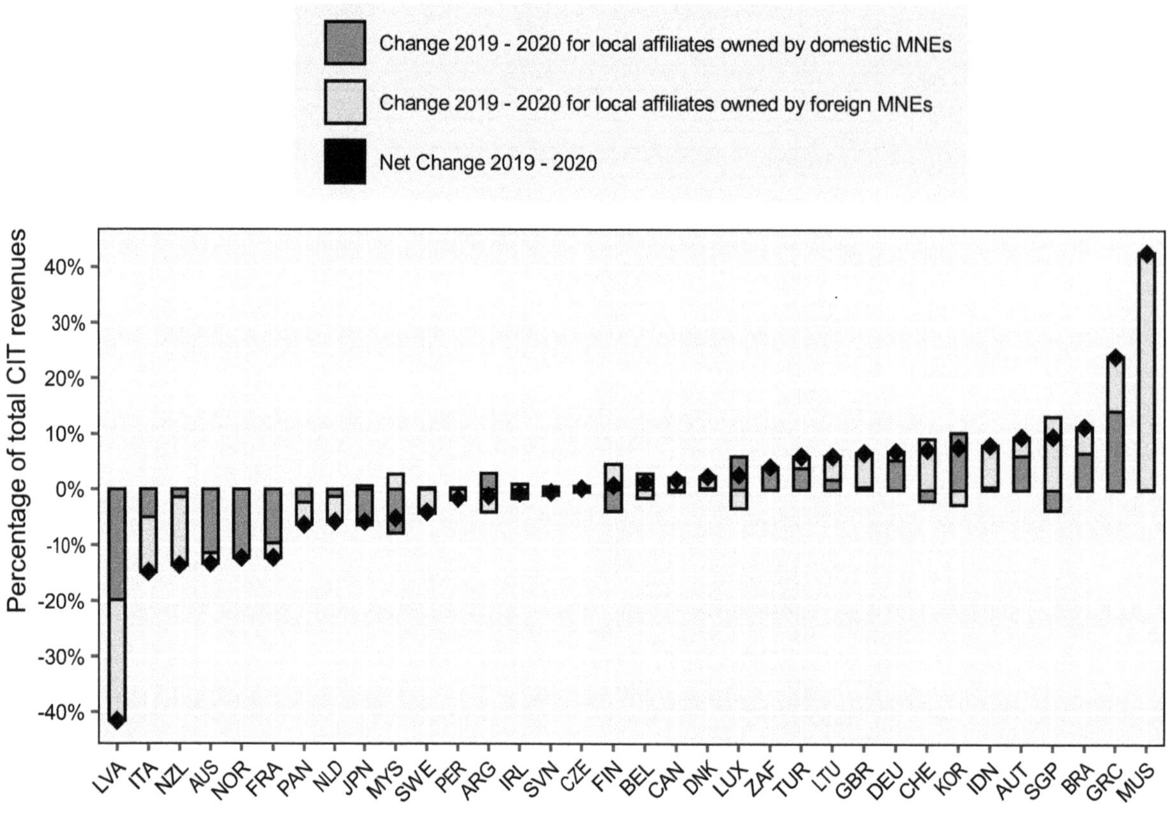

Source: Anonymised and Aggregated CbCR statistics and the OECD Global Revenue Statistics Database.

StatLink https://stat.link/gl9jiw

Figure 5.6. Domestic and foreign activities

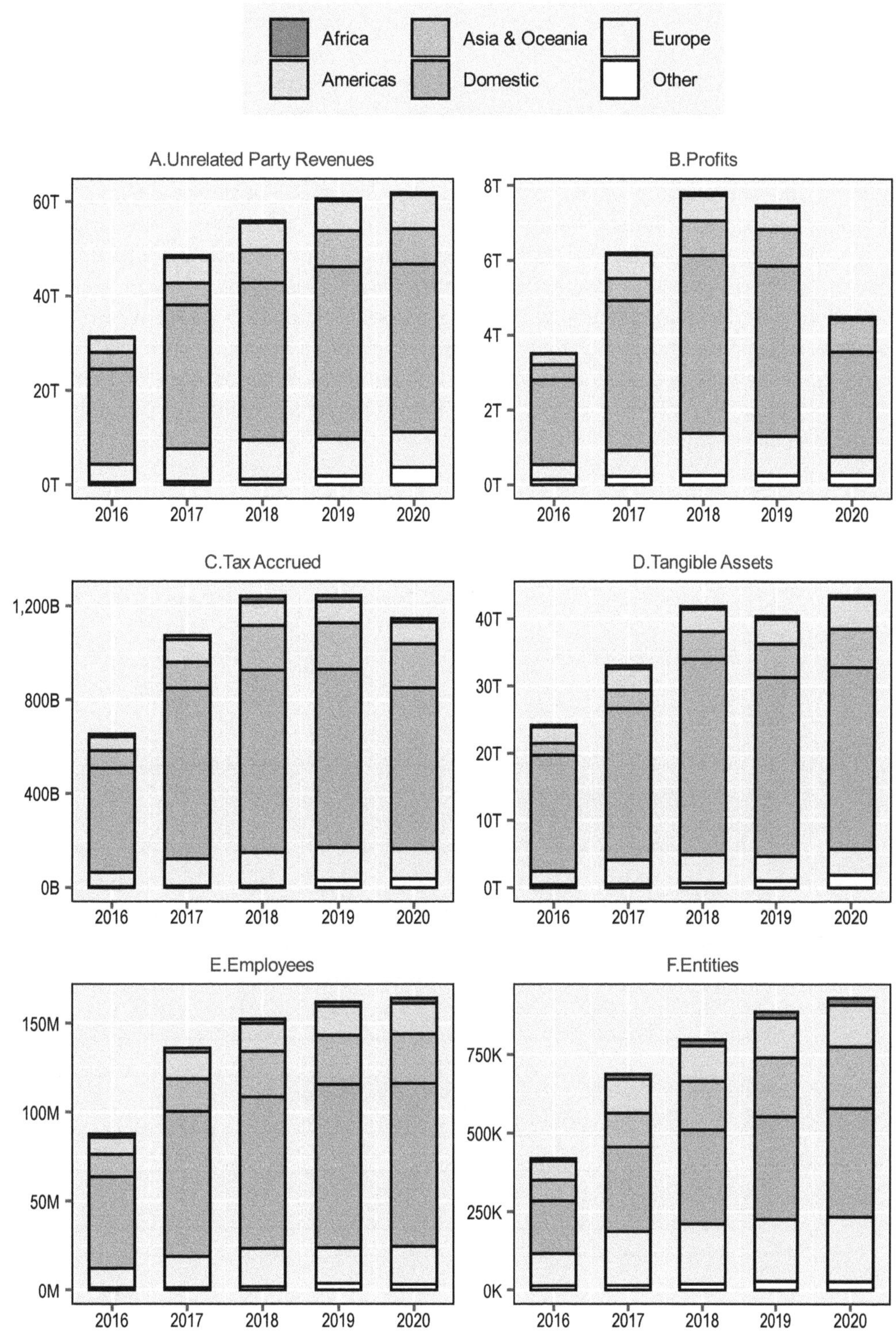

Note: T = trillions, B = billions, M = millions, K = thousands
Source: Anonymised and Aggregated CbCR statistics. These data are based on Table 1A of the CbCR statistics.

StatLink https://stat.link/nijfa9

General observations from CbCR tables

The presence and prevalence of different types of business activities may vary across regions for different reasons, including among others, the level of development, the demographic structure, trade patterns, or macroeconomic conditions. The existence of BEPS practices may also alter such prevalence in a given region. Figure 5.7 provides an overview of the top three business activities disaggregated into five regional groups for the most recent year for which data is available (2018).

Sales, marketing and distribution accounts for around one fifth of total business activity in four of the five regional groupings (all except "Other"). In regions with a relatively high share of low- and middle-income countries such as Africa and Asia and Oceania, manufacturing or production is also a common business activity, accounting for around 13% of the total number of activities in each region. Europe is the only region where administrative, management, or support services is included in the top three (13.0%). Holding shares or other equity instruments and holding or managing intellectual property are the business activities that reach the top three only in the Other regional grouping which includes Stateless entities and those that were not disaggregated. This may be indicative of tax planning structures but could also be the result of genuine commercial activity.

Figure 5.7. Top three business activities by region

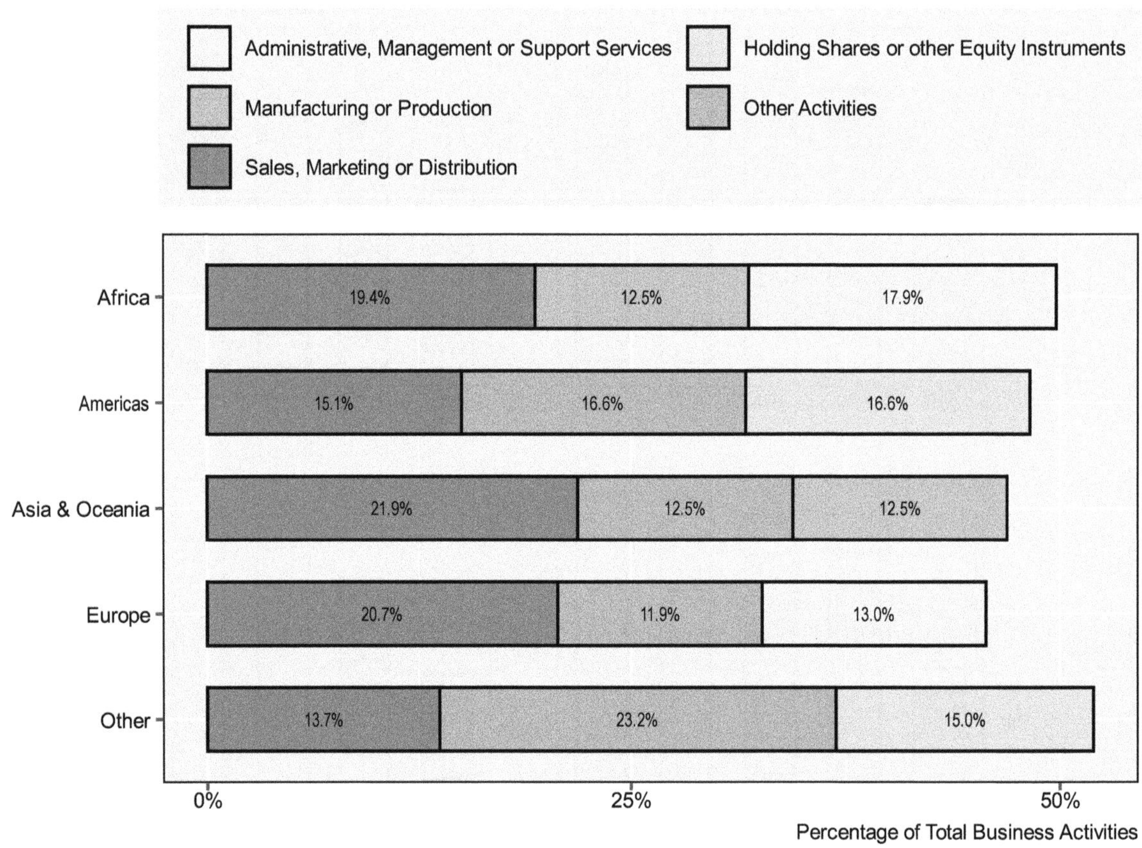

Source: 2020 Anonymised and Aggregated CbCR statistics. These data are based on the business activities data in Table 1A of the CbCR data.

StatLink https://stat.link/fm2x4o

Figure 5.8. Data disaggregated by the ETR of MNE Group

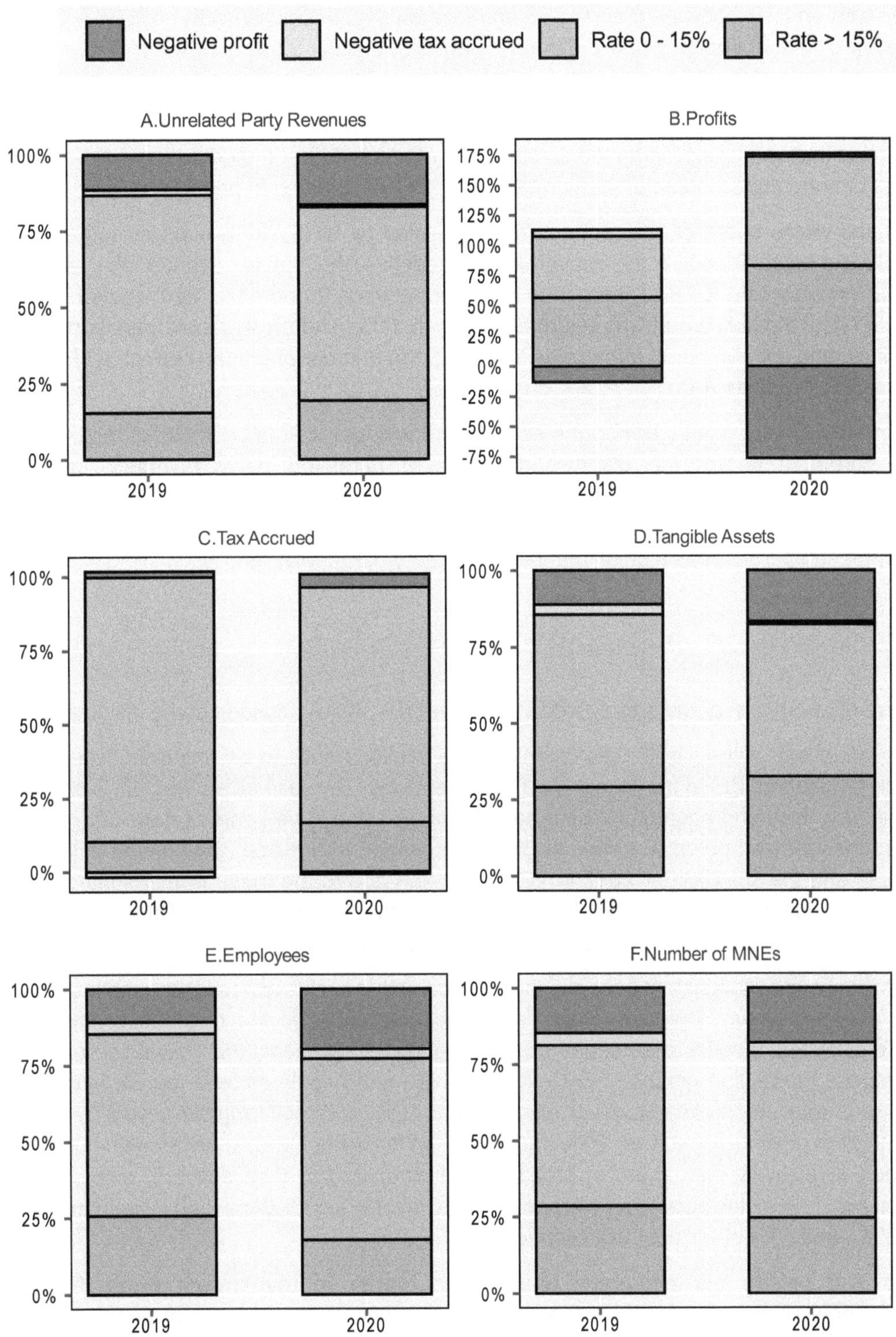

Source: 2019 and 2020 Anonymised and Aggregated CbCR statistics. These data are based on Table 4 of the CbCR statistics.

StatLink https://stat.link/fe5kj8

Figure 5.8 shows the share of different activities operated by MNEs disaggregated into four groups including MNEs for which the total profit was negative, the total tax accrued was negative, located in a jurisdiction with an ETR between 0 and 15%, and located in a jurisdiction with an ETR equal to or above 15%. The six available panels capture different statistics, including the number of MNEs (panel F), the number of employees (panel E), and selected financial variables (panels A-D).

The information shown in Figure 5.9 is the same as the one presented in Figure 5.8 except that the disaggregation into four groups is based on subgroup characteristics. In addition, panel F now represents the number of subgroups instead of the number of MNEs (as depicted in panel A above).

Figure 5.9 shows the share of different activities operated by MNE sub-groups disaggregated into four groups including MNEs for which the total profit was negative, the total tax accrued was negative, located in a jurisdiction where the ETR of the sub-group was between 0 and 15%, and located in a jurisdiction where the ETR of the sub-group was equal to or above 15%. The six available panels capture different statistics, including the number of subgroups (panel F), the number of employees (panel E), and selected financial variables (panels A-D).

The size of MNE groups varies across the sample and includes a small number of relatively large MNE groups. Figure 5.10 shows the distribution points of unrelated party revenues of MNE groups headquartered in each reporting jurisdiction. A common feature across all jurisdictions is that the mean MNE size in terms of unrelated party revenues is considerably larger than the median size, indicating that the underlying sample includes a small number of relatively large MNE groups.

Key insights on BEPS from CbCR data

This release of anonymised and aggregated CbCR data (FY 2020) provides some insights on BEPS.

Due to the limitations of the CbCR data, considerable caution needs to be exercised when attempting to draw conclusions about BEPS from the data. This is especially the case given that this is only the fifth year for which anonymised and aggregated data have been provided. Five years of data can give only limited insights on changes and potential trends in BEPS behaviour. In addition, the comparability between the 2016 sample and the samples for 2017 to 2020 is limited due to the move from voluntary to mandatory filing in some countries and differences in fiscal year coverage (see Box 5.2). Taking these caveats into account, the 2023 release of CbCR statistics suggests some insights on BEPS:

There is evidence of misalignment between the location where profits are reported and the location where economic activities occur. The data show continuing differences in the distribution across jurisdiction groups of employees, tangible assets, and profits.[9] Figure 5.11 presents the distribution of MNEs' foreign activities across jurisdiction groups.[10] For example, high and middle income jurisdictions account for a higher share of total employees (respectively 32% and 42%) and total tangible assets (respectively 32% and 32%) than of profits (respectively 25% and 14%). On the other hand, in investment hubs, on average, MNEs report a relatively high share of profits (30%) compared to their share of employees (4%) and tangible assets (11%). High income jurisdictions, middle income jurisdictions, and investment hubs account for 32%, 32%, and 10% of tax accrued, respectively.[11]

Revenues and profits per employee tend to be higher in investment hubs. Figure 5.12 and Figure 5.13 shows how the ratio of total revenues and profits to the number of employees is higher in investment hubs. In investment hubs, median revenues per employee are USD 1 710 000 while in high-, middle- and low-income jurisdictions median revenues per employee are USD 460 000, USD 195 000 and USD 160 000 respectively. While this may reflect differences in capital intensity or in worker productivity, it is likely also at least partially an indicator of BEPS.

Figure 5.9. Data disaggregated by the ETR of MNE sub-group

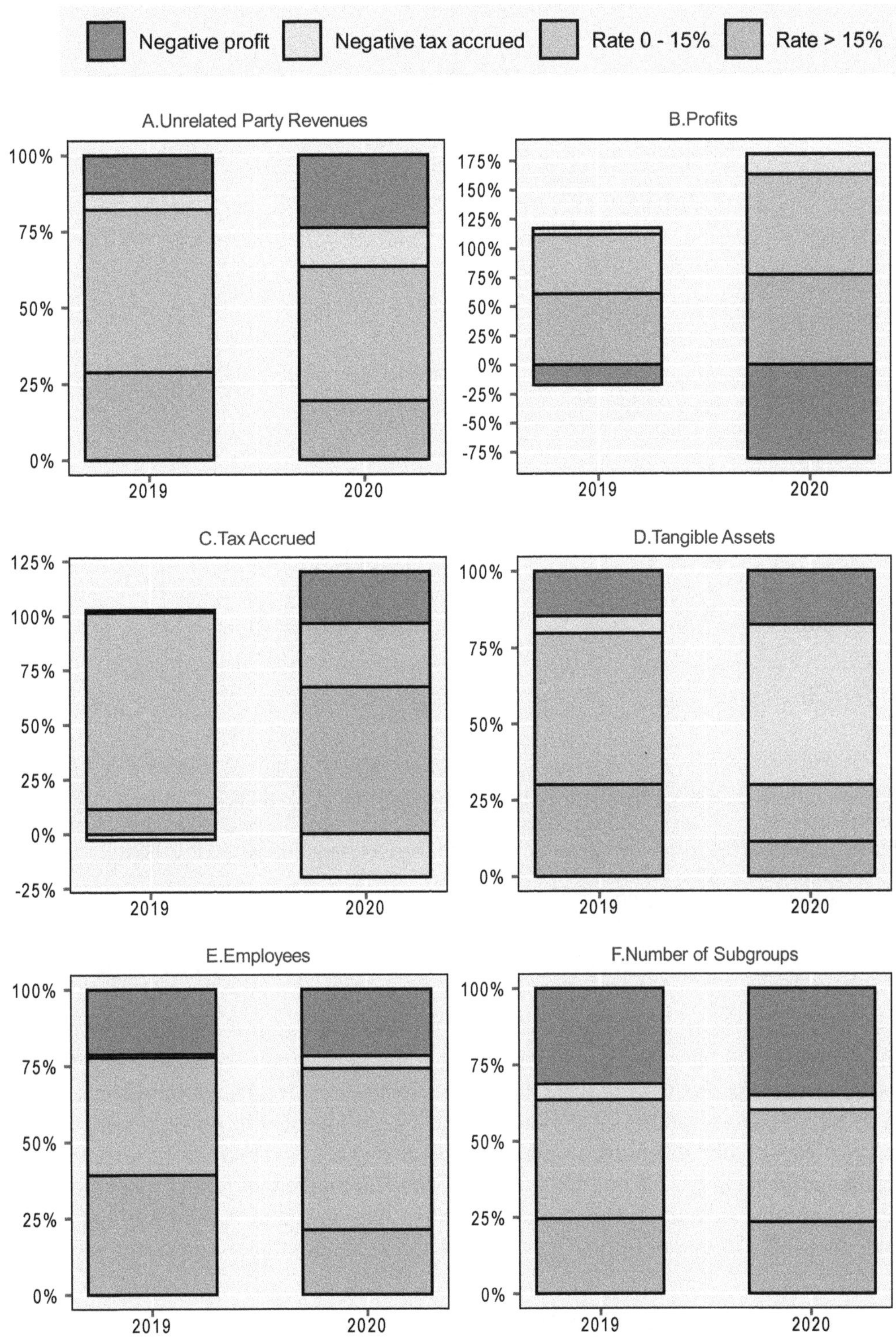

Source: Source: 2019 and 2020 Anonymised and Aggregated CbCR statistics. These data are based on Table 5 of the CbCR statistics.

StatLink https://stat.link/3zecu5

Figure 5.10. Distribution of MNE unrelated party revenues by ultimate parent jurisdiction

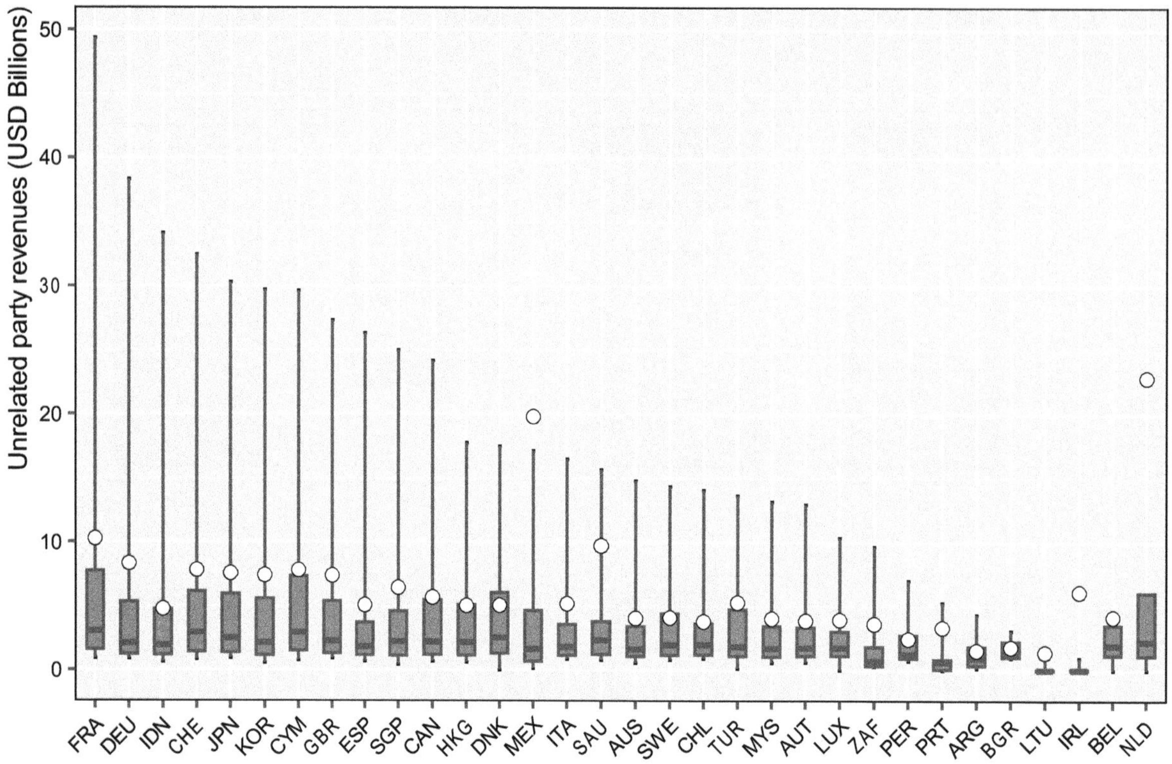

Note: The white dot represents the average value (obtained by dividing totals by the number of CbCRs), the blue boxes are delimited by the 25th and 75th percentiles, thus representing 50% of the sample within each jurisdiction. The horizontal black bar shows the median (50th percentile). The two whiskers indicate the 5th and 95th percentiles. Jurisdictions are ranked with respect to the 95th percentile where available. Country coverage reflects data availability in Table 6 of the CbCR data.
Source: 2020 Anonymised and Aggregated CbCR statistics.

StatLink https://stat.link/obsazv

On average, the share of related party revenues in total revenues is higher for MNEs in certain jurisdictions. Figure 5.14 plots the distribution of related party revenues as a share of total revenues, by jurisdiction group. On average, the share of related party revenues in total revenues is higher in investment hubs than in high-, middle- and low-income jurisdictions. In investment hubs, related party revenues account for over 30% of total revenues, whereas the median share of related party revenues in high-, and middle-income jurisdictions is 18% and 13% respectively. The median share of related party revenues in low-income jurisdictions is much lower at just 5%. While high levels of related party revenues may be commercially motivated, they are also a high-level risk assessment factor and could be evidence of tax planning.

The composition of business activity differs across jurisdiction groups. Figure 5.15 shows the share of main business activities in each jurisdiction group. In high-, middle- and low-income jurisdictions, sales, manufacturing, and services are the most prevalent activities, while in investment hubs the predominant activity is "holding shares" which also includes other equity instruments. A concentration of holding companies is a risk assessment factor and could be indicative of certain tax planning structures. However, as with related party revenues, this observation may also relate to genuine commercial arrangements.

Figure 5.11. Jurisdiction groups' shares of foreign MNEs' activities

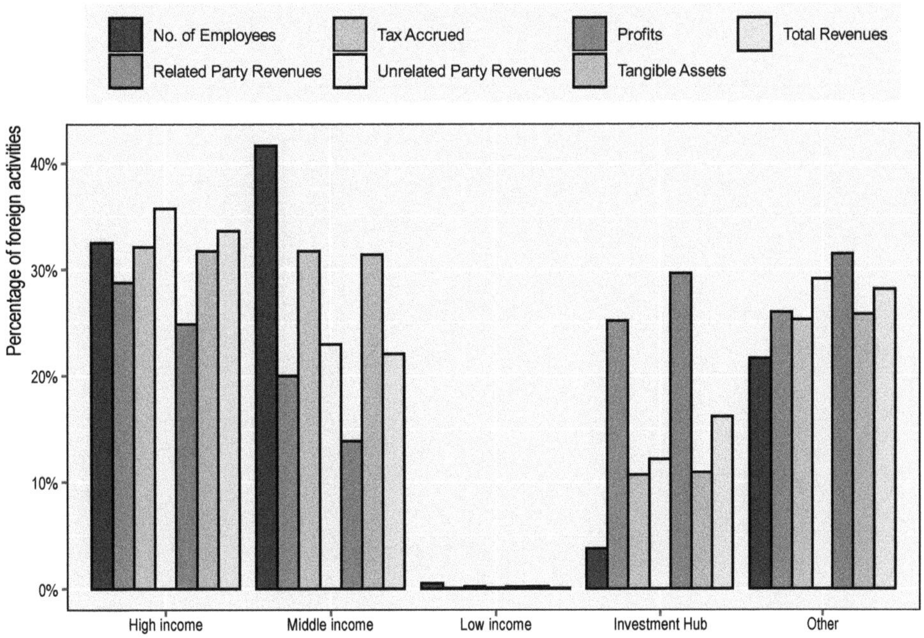

Note: The profit variable could include intracompany dividends in several instances and therefore be upward biased. The bars represent jurisdiction groups' shares of different variables (e.g., profit in group x/total profits booked in foreign jurisdictions) across all jurisdictions included in the CbCR sample. The percentages are calculated using Table 1A Panel A (all subgroups). "Other" reflects aggregate geographic groupings and Stateless entities.
Source: 2020 Anonymised and Aggregated CbCR statistics.

StatLink https://stat.link/bt1elp

Figure 5.12. Median profits per employee: distribution within jurisdiction groups

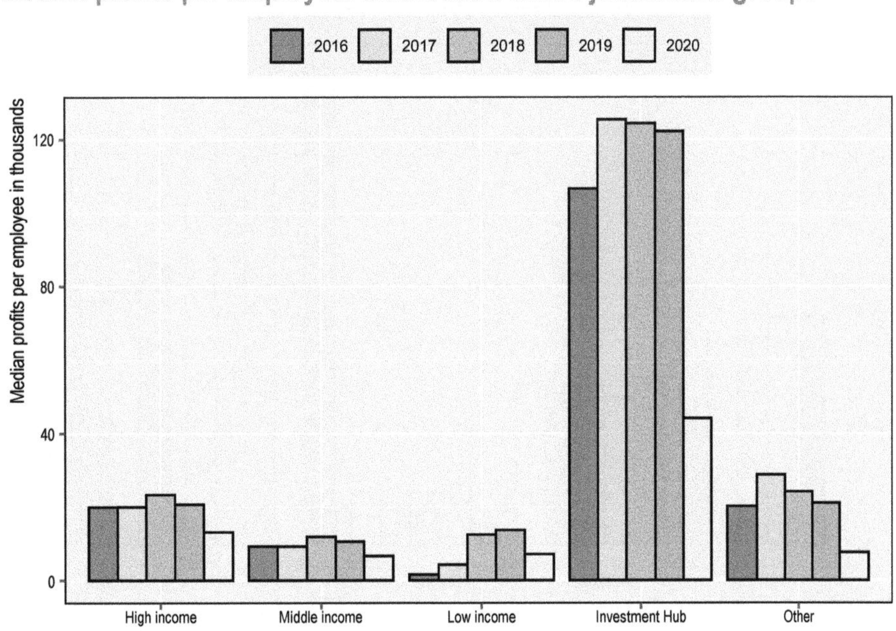

Note: "Other" reflects aggregate geographic groupings and Stateless entities.
Source: Anonymised and Aggregated CbCR statistics.

StatLink https://stat.link/2hcipq

Figure 5.13. Median total revenues per employee: Distribution within jurisdiction groups

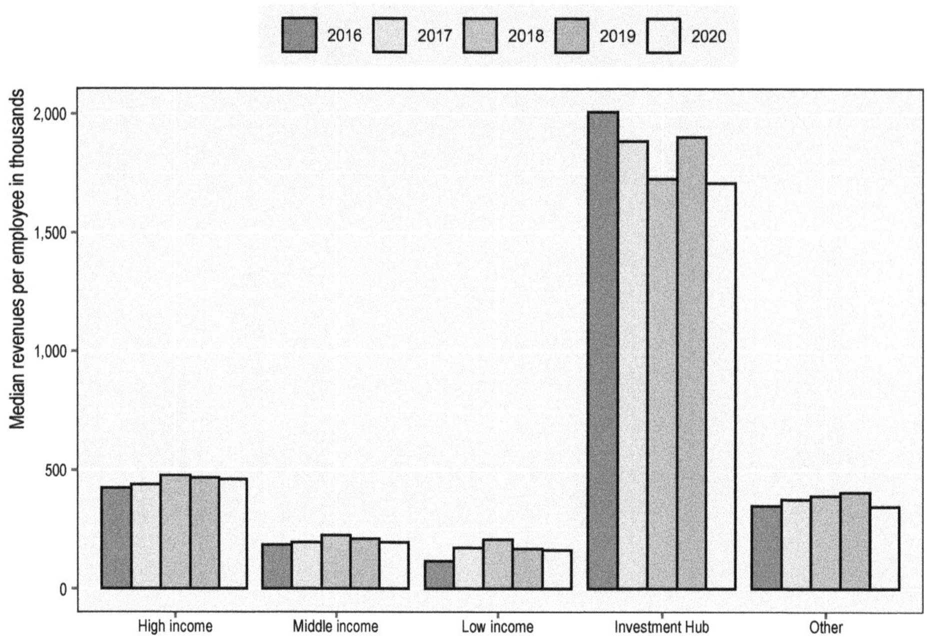

Note: "Other" reflects aggregate geographic groupings and Stateless entities.
Source: 2020 Anonymised and Aggregated CbCR statistics.

StatLink https://stat.link/cuojzf

Figure 5.14. Median related party revenues shares: Distribution within jurisdiction groups

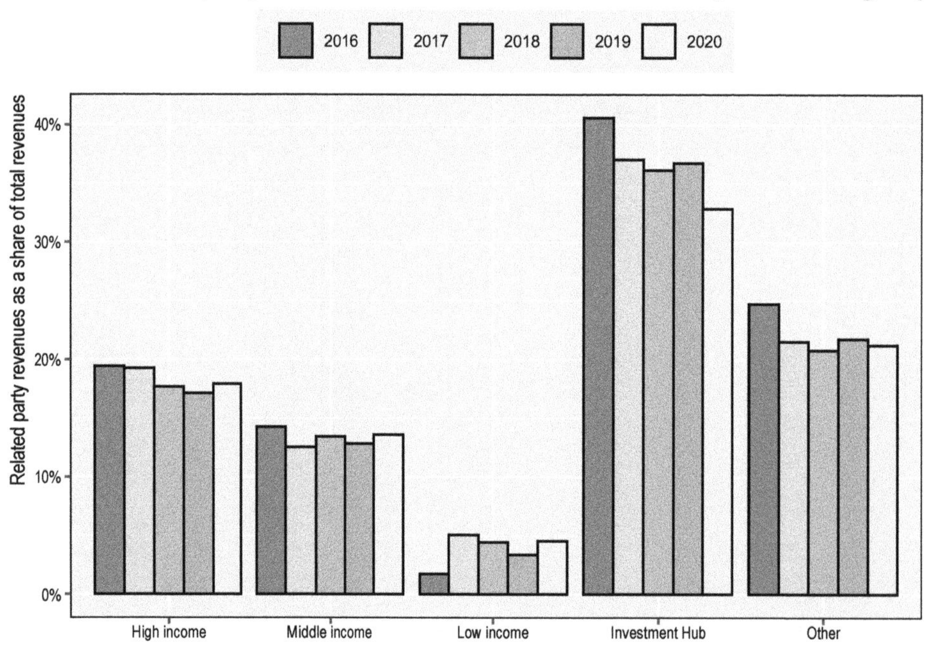

Note: The chart displays the distribution of related party revenues as a share of total revenues within each jurisdiction group. "Other" reflects aggregate geographic groupings and Stateless entities.
Source: 2020 Anonymised and Aggregated CbCR statistics.

StatLink https://stat.link/5gj76c

Figure 5.15. Top three business activities performed in jurisdiction groups

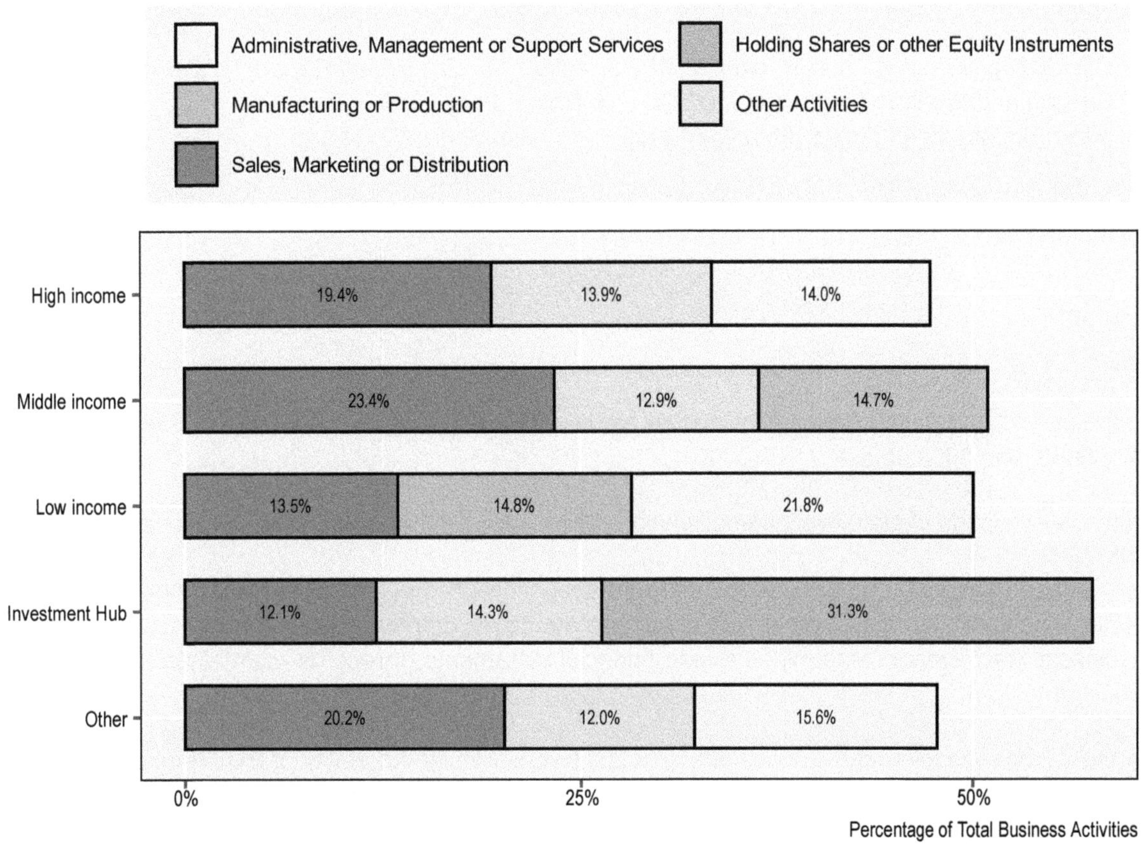

Note: The ratios are calculated by dividing the number of the activities performed in a jurisdiction group by the total number of all activities performed in this jurisdiction group where data is available. For example, 20% of all activities performed in high income jurisdictions are in the "sales" category. Entities could be attributed to one or more of the following activities: research and development; holding or managing intellectual property; purchasing or procurement; manufacturing or production (manufacturing); sales, marketing or distribution (sales); administrative, management or support services; provision of services to unrelated parties (services); internal group finance; regulated financial services; insurance; holding shares or other equity instruments (holding shares); dormant; other activities. For the United States, other activities also include holding or managing intellectual property; insurance; internal group finance; and research and development.
Source: 2020 Anonymised and Aggregated CbCR statistics

StatLink https://stat.link/qzt6un

References

OECD (2015), *Measuring and Monitoring BEPS, Action 11 - 2015 Final Report*, OECD/G20 Base Erosion and Profit Shifting Project, OECD Publishing, Paris, https://doi.org/10.1787/9789264241343-en. [1]

Notes

[1] In the case of the United States, CbCR data are less granular than Inland Revenue Service (IRS) Form 5471, 8865, and 8858 data.

[2] With the exception of stateless income, which could relate to either domestic or foreign activities.

[3] Reporting MNEs may choose to use data from consolidation reporting packages, from separate entity statutory financial statements, regulatory financial statements, or internal management accounts. In some jurisdictions, taxpayers are permitted to use financial statements or records maintained for tax reporting purposes.

[4] In the European Union, the Council directive 2011/96/EU limits the ability of EU Member States to tax received dividends in order to exempt dividends and other profit distributions paid by subsidiary companies to their parent companies from withholding taxes and to eliminate double taxation of such income at the level of the parent company.

[5] Country specific analysis undertaken by Ireland, Italy, the Netherlands, Sweden and the United Kingdom are available at: Ireland: https://oe.cd/3Kn; Italy: https://oe.cd/3Ko; Netherlands: https://oe.cd/3Kp; Sweden: https://oe.cd/3Kq; United Kingdom: https://oe.cd/3Kr.

[6] The BEPS Action 13 report (http://www.oecd.org/tax/transfer-pricing-documentation-and-country-by-country-reporting-action-13-2015-final-report-9789264241480-en.htm) included a requirement that a review of the CbCR minimum standard be completed (the 2020 review). A public consultation meeting on the 2020 review of BEPS Action 13 was held virtually on 12-13 May 2020, where external stakeholders had the opportunity to provide input on the ongoing work.

[7] The 2017 data and future releases cover fiscal years ending between 1 January and 31 December of the respective year while the 2016 data contains CbCRs for fiscal years starting between 1 January and 1 July 2016.

[8] Foreign MNEs' contributions might be understated for two main reasons: first, some jurisdictions provided limited geographical disaggregation; second, the contributions of MNEs with parents headquartered in jurisdictions that did not provide data are missing.

[9] As indicated in Box 5.2, and described in greater detail at http://www.oecd.org/tax/tax-policy/anonymised-and-aggregated-cbcr-statistics-disclaimer.pdf, profits may be overestimated due to the inclusion of intra-company dividends. To evaluate the potential magnitude of included dividends country specific analyses

are available at: Netherlands: https://oe.cd/3Kp; Ireland: https://oe.cd/3Kn; Italy: https://oe.cd/3Ko; Sweden: https://oe.cd/3Kq; United Kingdom: https://oe.cd/3Kr.

[10] Jurisdiction groups (high, middle and low income) are based on the World Bank classification resulting in 61 high income jurisdictions, 104 middle income jurisdictions, and 29 low-income jurisdictions. Investment hubs are defined as jurisdictions with a total inward Foreign Direct Investment (FDI) position above 150% of gross domestic product (GDP).

[11] Tax accrued depends on both effective tax rates and taxable profits in a jurisdiction.

6 Intellectual property regimes

Key insights

- Forty-three regimes were found to be not harmful, and one was found to be harmful. Seven regimes were in the process of being amended or eliminated since they were not compliant with the base erosion and profit shifting (BEPS) Action 5 minimum standard. Eight regimes were abolished in 2023 and one regime was under review even though it had not yet been determined whether they were in compliance with the Action 5 minimum standard.
- Of the 43 non-harmful intellectual property (IP) regimes, all 43 offer benefits to patents, 32 offer benefits to copyrighted software and 19 offer benefits to the third allowed category of assets that are restricted to small and medium-sized enterprises (SMEs).
- Tax rate reductions for the 43 non-harmful IP regimes range from a full exemption from tax to a reduction of about 40% of the standard tax rate.
- All seven regimes that are in the process of being amended or eliminated offer a full exemption from taxation for IP income.

The *Corporate Tax Statistics* database also includes information on IP regimes. Many jurisdictions have implemented IP regimes, which allow income from the exploitation of certain IP assets to be taxed at a lower rate than the standard statutory tax rate (STR).

IP regimes may be used by governments to support research and development (R&D) activities in their jurisdiction. In the past, IP regimes may have been designed in a manner that incentivised firms to locate IP assets in a jurisdiction regardless of where the underlying R&D was undertaken. However, the nexus approach of the BEPS Action 5 minimum standard now requires that tax benefits for IP income are made conditional on the extent to which a taxpayer has undertaken the R&D activities that produced the IP asset in the jurisdiction providing the tax benefits.

Intellectual property regimes

The information reported for each IP regime in the *Corporate Tax Statistics* database is:

- the name of the regime;
- the qualifying IP assets;
- the reduced rate that applies under the IP regime;
- the status of the IP regime as determined by the OECD's Forum on Harmful Tax Practices (FHTP).

The Corporate Tax Statistics database draws on the detailed information collected by the FHTP for its peer reviews of preferential tax regimes. The information and the status presented are correct as of June 2023. Changes to regimes that have been legislated in 2023 but are not effective until 2024 are not reflected in this edition of the database.

The information presented in this edition provides a basic description of the IP regimes in place in 2023. Future editions will incorporate the effects of IP regimes into the corporate effective tax rate analysis.

Reduced rates available under non-harmful IP regimes ranged from 0% to 18.75% in 2023. The magnitude of the reductions ranges from around 40% to a full exemption from tax.

What qualifies as an intellectual property regime?

IP regimes can be regimes that exclusively provide benefits to income from IP, but some regimes categorised as IP regimes are "dual category" regimes. These regimes also provide benefits to income from other geographically mobile activities or to a wide range of activities and do not necessarily exclude income from IP.

The Corporate Tax Statistics database shows information both on regimes that narrowly target IP income and on regimes that offer reduced rates to IP income and other types of income. Of the 61 IP regimes contained in the database, 34 were reviewed by the FHTP as IP regimes only and 27 were reviewed as "dual category" regimes (IP and non-IP regimes).

Status of intellectual property regimes

On the basis of the features of the regime, IP regimes are found to be either: harmful (because they do not meet the nexus approach), not harmful (when the regime does meet the nexus approach and other factors in the review process), or potentially harmful (when the regime does not meet the nexus approach and/or other factors in the review process, but an assessment of the economic effects has not yet taken place). The peer review process is ongoing, and by 2023 the vast majority of regimes were fully aligned with the Action 5 minimum standard. These are listed with the status "Not harmful" or "not harmful (amended)". Regimes that were already closed to new entrants in 2023 (according to the peer reviews approved by the Inclusive Framework in June 2023) were listed as "abolished" in the database, although continuing benefits may be offered for a defined period of time to companies already benefiting from the regime. In most cases, this grandfathering would end by 30 June 2024. There were eight IP regimes abolished in 2023.

The Corporate Tax Statistics database contains information on 61 IP regimes that were in place in 46 different jurisdictions in the year 2022. Forty-three regimes in total were found to be not harmful; 26 of these regimes were found to be not harmful after having been amended to align with the Action 5 minimum standard. One regime (in Trinidad and Tobago) was found to be harmful. Seven regimes are in the process of being amended or eliminated since they were not compliant with the BEPS Action 5 minimum standard. One regime is under review, since it has not yet been determined whether it meets the Action 5 minimum standard. This can be the case with newly introduced IP regimes and IP regimes of jurisdictions that have recently joined the Inclusive Framework.

Figure 6.1. Status of intellectual property regimes in place in 2023

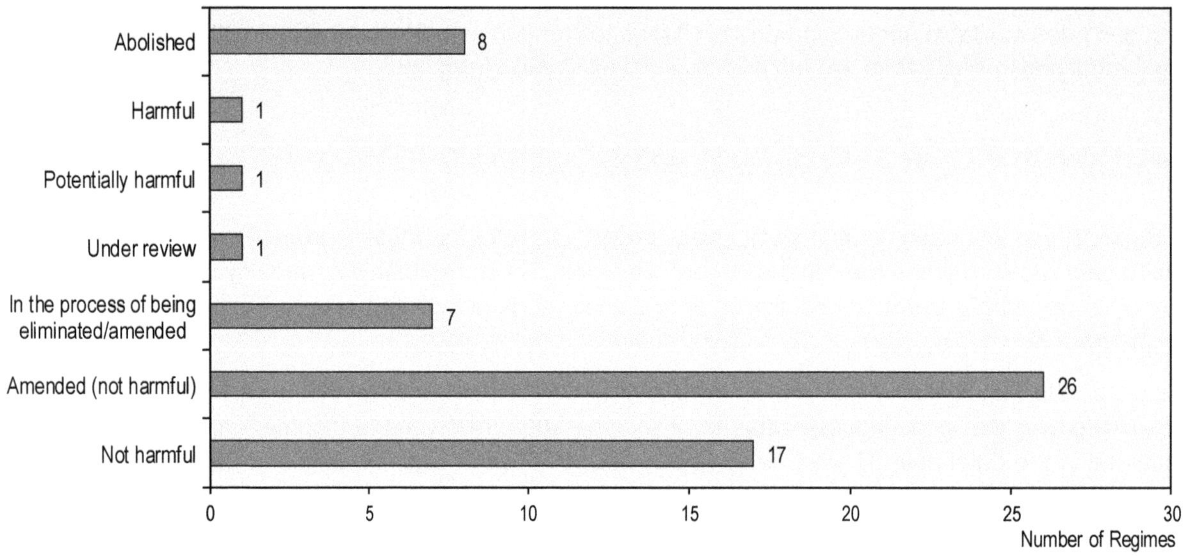

StatLink https://stat.link/vi6bgq

Qualifying assets and reduced tax rates

In the Corporate Tax Statistics database, qualifying assets of IP regimes are grouped into three main categories: patents, software and Category 3. These correspond to the only three categories of assets that may qualify for benefits under the Action 5 minimum standard: 1) patents defined broadly; 2) copyrighted software; and 3) in certain circumstances and only for SMEs, other IP assets that are non-obvious, useful and novel. The Action 5 Report explicitly excludes income from marketing related intangibles (such as trademarks) from benefiting from a tax preference. If a regime does not meet the Action 5 minimum standard, then the assets qualifying for the regime may not fall into the three allowed categories.

Of the 43 regimes found to be not harmful, all 43 regimes cover patents, 32 cover software, and 19 regimes cover assets in the third category (Category 3). All seven regimes that are in the process of being eliminated or amended do not have any restrictions on the type of income that qualifies for a reduced rate, although there may be restrictions to certain industries or income types. The reduction in the rate on IP income varies among the regimes, and some regimes offer different rates depending, for example, on the type of income (e.g., royalties or capital gains income) or size of the company.

Among the 43 regimes found to be not harmful, the tax benefit offered ranges from a full exemption to a reduction of about 40% of the tax rate that would have otherwise applied. The most common reduction is a 50% reduction. The reduced rates range from 0% (in 13 jurisdictions) to 18.75% (Korea's Special taxation for transfer, acquisition, etc. of technology; this IP regime offers reduced rates ranging from 5% to 18.75%). All seven regimes that are in the process of being amended or eliminated offer a full exemption from taxation for IP income.

For each of the 43 non-harmful IP regimes, Figure 6.2 and Figure 6.3 show the lowest reduced rate offered under the regime and the tax rate that would otherwise apply. Figure 6.2 shows those regimes with the status non-harmful, while Figure 6.3 shows the regimes that have been amended to be non-harmful. The tax rate that would otherwise apply is typically the STR, but it may not include certain surtaxes or sub-central government taxes. Similar to the reduced rate, the tax rate that would otherwise apply may also fall into a range, for example, if the standard statutory rate depends on the level of profits. Therefore, the tax rates shown in the figures are representative and do not detail the full range of tax reductions offered in each IP regime.

Figure 6.2. Reduced rates under non-harmful intellectual property regimes, 2023

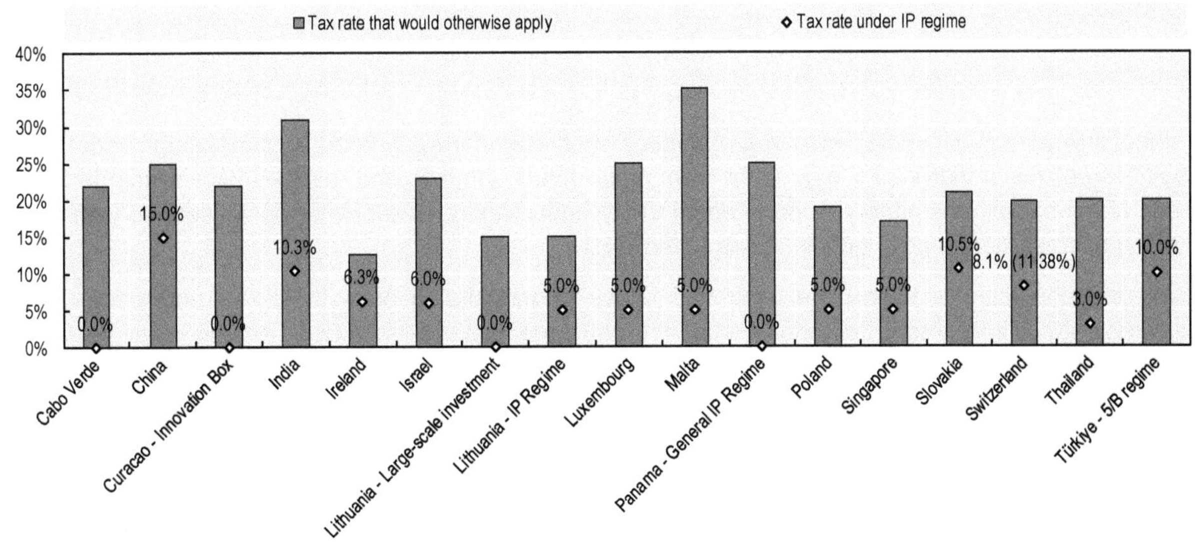

Note: IP income in Switzerland can benefit from a 90% exemption of qualifying IP income from cantonal taxation. However, this exemption is subject to a cap: only 70% of a firm's total profits (IP or non-IP) can be exempt. The canton of Zurich is chosen as the representative canton. The 8.11% in 2023 applies to qualifying IP income and assumes that the firm has sufficient other income (non-qualifying IP or non-IP income) that is taxed at higher rates so that it is not subject to the 70% maximum relief limitation. If the firm had enough qualifying IP income that the 70% maximum relief limitation did apply, the rate applied to IP income in the city of Zurich would increase steadily from 8.11% to 11.38% in 2023 (100% IP Income). Where multiple rates are available for royalties or capital gains, the rate applicable to royalties has been used.

StatLink https://stat.link/jnwb75

Figure 6.3. Reduced rates under non-harmful (amended) intellectual property regimes, 2023

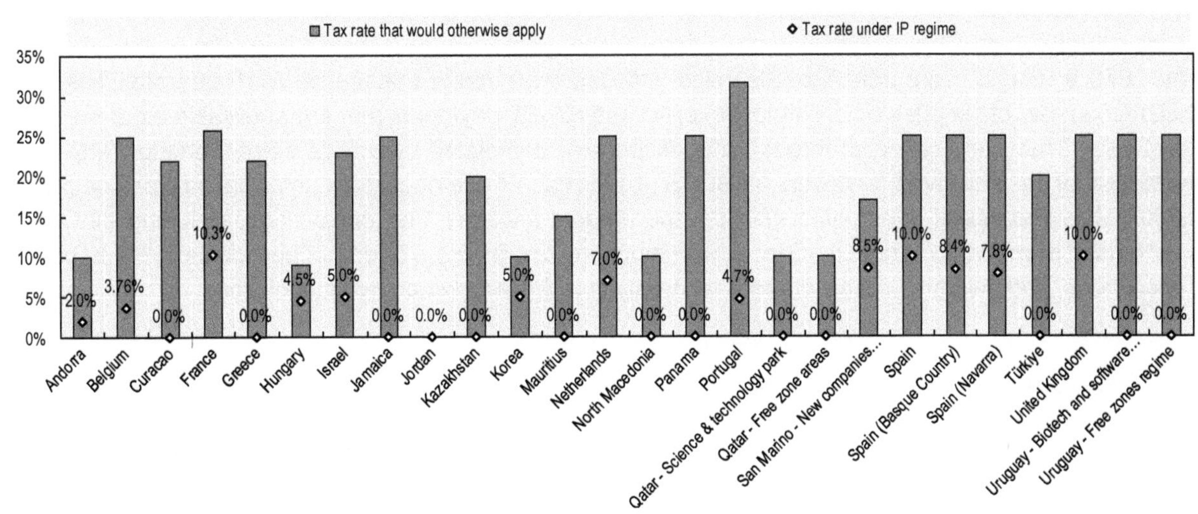

Note: Where multiple rates are available for royalties or capital gains, the rate applicable to royalties has been used.

StatLink https://stat.link/fga2et

7 Withholding tax rates

Withholding taxes (WHTs) are levied on businesses when they make payments to other foreign or domestic business entities or individuals, e.g., in the form of dividends, interest, and royalties. Governments collect these taxes based on statutory or preferential treaty-based tax rates requiring businesses to withhold a fraction of cross-border payments in scope of the WHT.

Data on withholding taxes can be used to improve understanding of multinational enterprise (MNE) decisions about investment, repatriation, finance and organisational structures among other tax policy issues. For example:

- WHTs increase the cost of repatriating profits earned in foreign jurisdictions thereby potentially discouraging MNEs' investment decisions at the extensive margin (i.e., discrete investment decisions between two or more alternative projects);
- differences in WHT rates between interest and dividend payments, both within and across locations, could affect MNEs' financing decisions;
- taxes levied on cross-border payments increase the cost of capital and could thus affect investments at the intensive margin (i.e., the incentive to expand existing investments given a fixed location). (Auerbach, Devereux and Simpson, 2008[10])

Importantly, WHT data can also potentially provide insights on certain base erosion and profit shifting (BEPS) strategies such as treaty shopping or the strategic location of debt and intangible assets. The publication of WHT rates in Corporate Tax Statistics was envisaged in the 2015 BEPS Action 11 Report (OECD, 2015[1]).

General data characteristics

The 2023 edition of Corporate Tax Statistics includes the second release of WHT rate statistics. The dataset consists of tax rates on dividends, interest and royalty payments that are applicable as of the 2023 fiscal year. They were collected through a questionnaire completed by delegates of Working Party No.2 meeting in of the Inclusive Framework on BEPS (IF) format. Where necessary, information was completed using public sources of information. In total, the dataset includes 119 jurisdictions, including all OECD members. It is important to note that baseline withholding tax rates are often not applicable to cross-border transactions, particularly in cases where a tax treaty is in force between two jurisdictions.

Withholding tax rates across jurisdictions

Figure 7.1 displays the average standard withholding tax rates applicable for dividends, interest, and royalty payments across the 119 IF jurisdictions covered. Jurisdictions are categorised in three groups: high income jurisdictions, low and middle-income jurisdictions and investment hubs.[1] Figure 7.1 shows that the ranking of average standard WHT rates varies across jurisdiction groups. On average, low and middle-income jurisdictions levy higher WHT rates on royalty payments while high income jurisdictions and investment hubs levy higher rates on interest. In particular, the following can be observed:

- **Dividends:** High income jurisdictions levy an average standard WHT on dividends of 15.5%, which is 4.3 p.p. larger than the average standard WHT rate on dividends in low and middle-income jurisdictions (11.2%) and about three times larger than the average rate in investment hubs (5.2%).
- **Interest:** Concerning interest payments, the average standard WHT rate in high income jurisdictions is 11.8% compared to 15.9% in low and middle-income jurisdictions and 4.8% in investment hubs.
- **Royalties:** Royalty payments are subject to an average standard WHT rate of 15.6% in high income jurisdictions and 16.6% in low and middle-income jurisdictions. These rates are considerably higher than the average standard 3.6% WHT rate applied to royalties in investment hubs.

Figure 7.1. Average withholding tax rates: Dividends, interest, and royalties, 2023

Investment hubs, low and middle income, and high-income jurisdictions

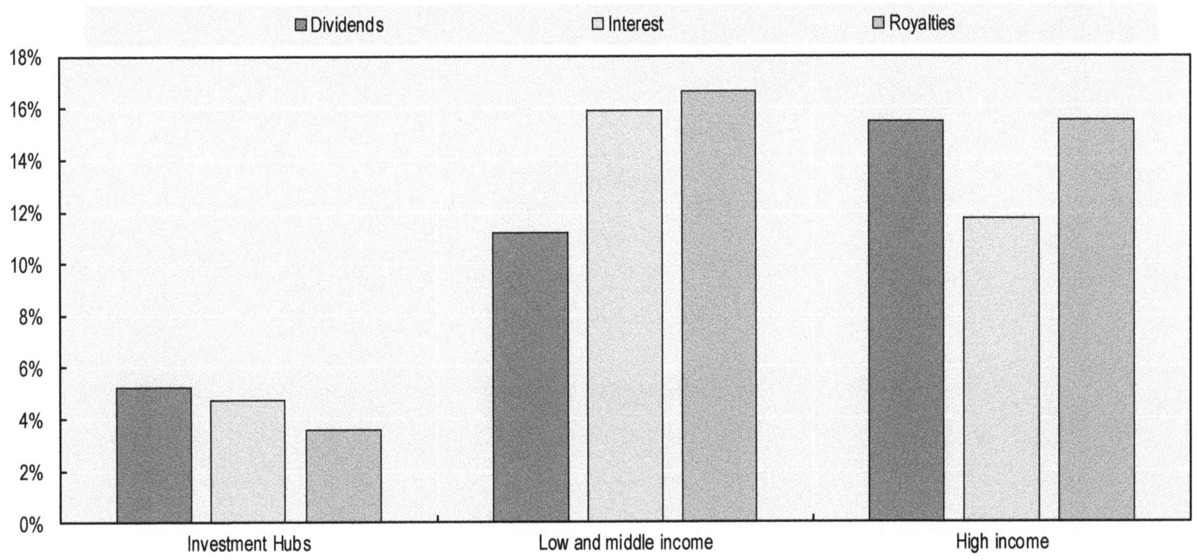

StatLink https://stat.link/4t06wz

Figure 7.2 depicts the density ratios of WHT rates for the three jurisdiction groups along four ranges of WHT rates. Density ratios capture the number of jurisdictions that levy a standard WHT rate in each range, as a share (expressed in p.p.) of the total number of jurisdictions in the dataset. Ratios are presented separately for each jurisdiction group as well as for each cross-border payment type. Panel A of Figure 7.2 shows the distribution of ratios for WHTs on cross-border dividend payments. Three quarters of the investment hubs covered in the dataset levy a WHT on dividends at a standard rate below 10%. This includes, among others, Anguilla (0.0%), Cyprus (0.0%), and Singapore (0.0%). Fourteen per cent of investment hubs levy a WHT on dividends at a standard rate between 10% and 20%.

The remaining jurisdictions are Ireland and Switzerland, which levy a WHT on dividends at standard rates of 25.0% and 35.0%, respectively. Among low and middle-income jurisdictions, more than half levy a WHT on dividends at a standard rate between 10% and 20%. Thirteen of the 49 jurisdictions in this group have standard WHT rates below 10%, including Brazil (0.0%) and Peru (5.0%). Of the low and middle-income jurisdictions, only Jamaica (33.3%) has a standard WHT rate on dividends above 20%. The largest share of high-income jurisdictions (about one third) levy WHTs on dividends at standard rates below 10%. This includes the United Kingdom (0.0%), Greece (5.0%), and Uruguay (7.0%), among others. In the remaining three ranges of standard WHT rates above 10%, the number of high-income jurisdictions is between 9 and 12 jurisdictions for each range. At the top-end of the distribution are jurisdictions such as Chile (35.0%),

Czechia (35.0%), and Greenland (44.0%). As mentioned above, these rates do not account for any tax treaties that may exist.

Figure 7.2. Density ratios of WHT rates: Dividends, interest, and royalties, 2023

Investment hubs, low and middle income, and high-income countries

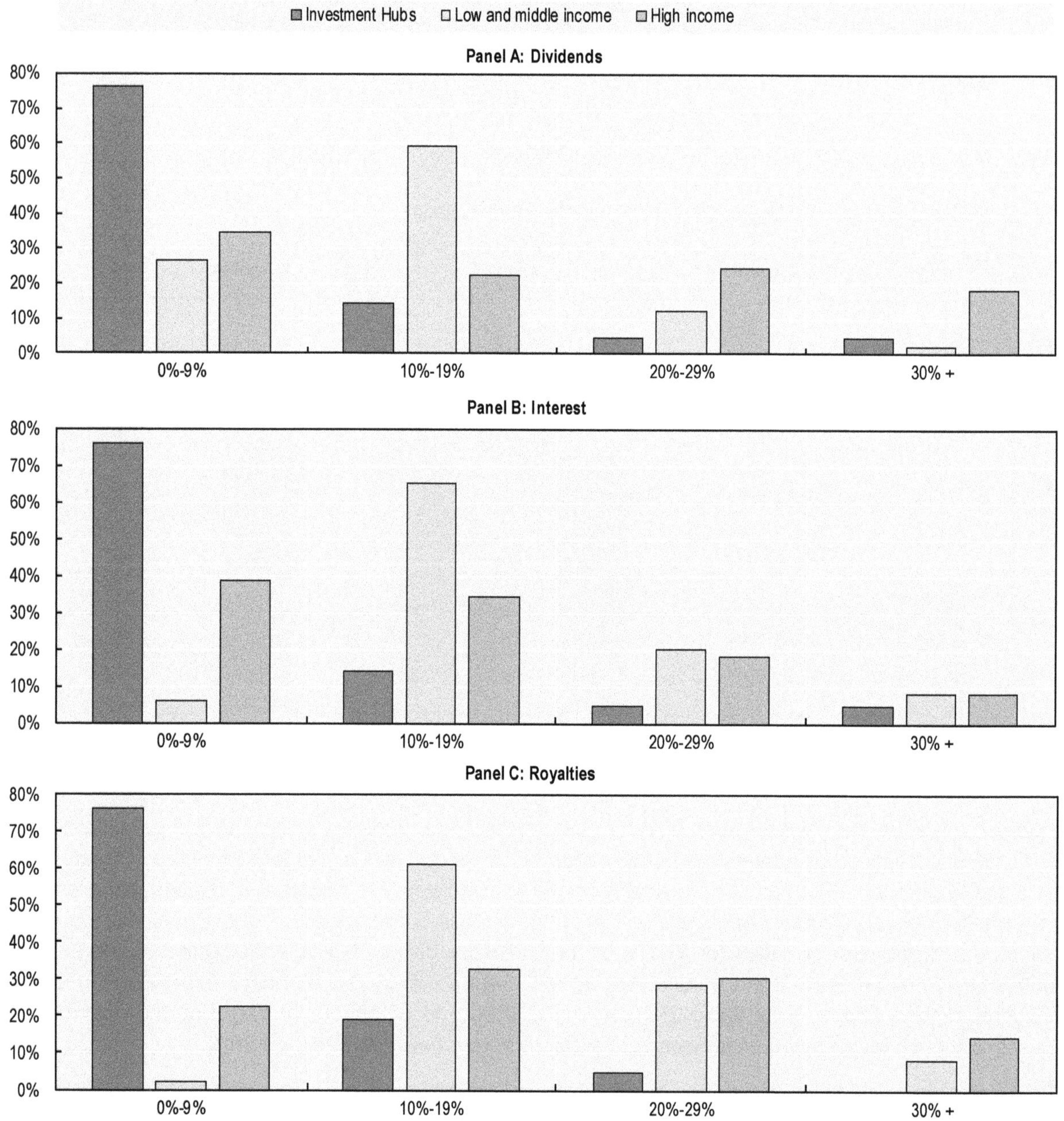

StatLink https://stat.link/8nb674

Panel B of Figure 7.2 presents the spread of density ratios applicable to cross-border interest payments. The majority of investment hubs (76% of the group) levy a WHT on interest at a standard rate below 10%. Among others, this includes Bermuda (0.0%), Malta (0.0%), and the Netherlands (0.0%). Of the remaining five investment hubs, Switzerland (35.0%) and Ireland (20%) are at the top of the distribution of standard rates. Over 65% of low and middle-income jurisdictions levy a WHT on interest at a standard rate between

10% and 20%. Three jurisdictions levy a WHT on interest at a standard rate lower than 10%, Paraguay (4.5%), Georgia (5.0%), and Viet Nam (5.0%). Four jurisdictions levy a WHT on interest at a rate greater than 30% including Peru (30.0%), Jamaica (33.3%), Argentina (35.0%) and Mexico (35.0%). High income jurisdictions are concentrated in the lower parts of the distribution, with 38.7% of high-income jurisdictions levying WHTs on interest at standard rates below 10%. In the higher tax brackets, 34.7% of jurisdictions levy WHTs on interest at standard rates between 10% and 20%, 22.5% between 20 and 30% group, and 8.1% above 30%. Liechtenstein (0.0%), Monaco (0.0%) and Sweden (0.0%) are three of the 19 jurisdictions among the high-income group that levy a WHT on interest at a standard rate below 10%. The highest standard WHT rate among high income jurisdictions is levied at the same rate (35.0%) in Chile and Czechia.

The distribution of density ratios of WHTs on cross-border royalty payments are found in Panel C of Figure 7.2. Most investment hubs have standard WHT rates on royalties below 10%. This range includes Hungary (0.0%), Jersey (0.0%), and Hong-Kong (5.0%), among others. The upper tail of the distribution of investment hubs consists of Liberia (15.0%), Mauritius (15.0%), and Ireland (20.0%). Royalty payments are subject to WHTs at standard rates between 10% and 20% in over half of the low and middle-income jurisdictions (61%). The lower end of the distribution in this group consists of Georgia and India which levy a WHT on royalties at a standard rate of 5.0% and 10% respectively. The upper end includes Peru (30.0%), Jamaica (33.3%), and Argentina (35.0%). Almost one third of the high-income group levies a WHT on royalties at a standard rate between 20% and 30%. Among the high-income jurisdictions that levy the lowest standard WHT rates are Aruba (0.0%), Latvia (0.0%), and the United Arab Emirates (0.0%). Belgium (30.0%), Italy (30.0%), and the United States (30.0%) are three of the seven jurisdictions that levy WHTs at a standard rate of 30% or above in this category.

Treaty-based withholding tax rates

Bilateral tax conventions can play a crucial role in encouraging and fostering economic ties between countries. They do so by reducing tax obstacles to cross-border services, trade and investment through the avoidance of double taxation, addressing excessive taxation, offering protection from discriminatory tax treatment of foreign investment and by providing greater certainty of tax treatment for taxpayers.

One way in which bilateral tax treaties achieve some of these aims is through the limitation of withholding taxes that may be applied certain income. This section provides data on the tax treaties amongst the jurisdictions covered in the database and provides additional details on the withholding tax rates on dividends, interest, royalties, and technical fees, that are applied as final withholding tax rates.[2]

The number of treaties has expanded significantly in recent years across the 131 jurisdictions in the dataset, with only 1000 treaties among these countries in 1990 compared to almost 4500 in 2023 Figure 7.3. However recent years have seen a levelling off of the expansion in tax treaties, with only 36 additional treaties included in the database during the period 2017-2023.[3] The modest increase in new bilateral treaties during this period does not mean that there has not still been significant treaty-related change; for example, many countries have signed the MLI, and many treaties have been amended by protocol.

The data suggest that countries outside the OECD have fewer treaties than OECD countries. Figure 7.4 shows that OECD countries have higher numbers of treaties on average than IF member jurisdictions in Africa and Latin American and the Caribbean, which contain more non-OECD member jurisdictions. Though all groups have seen significant growth in their average number of tax treaties, this growth has been strongest amongst OECD countries. The data show that treaty-based withholding tax rates are substantially lower than withholding tax rates applicable under domestic law. Overall, Figure 7.5 shows that treaty-based withholding tax rates show a substantial mass of rates below 5%.

Figure 7.3. Number of bilateral treaties, 1990-2023

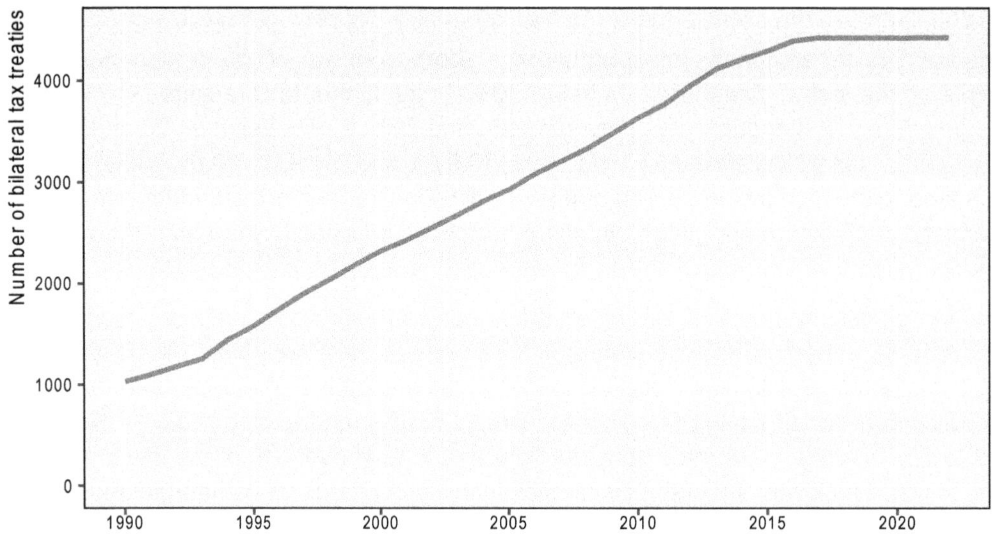

Note: Data are based on bilateral treaties reported by 131 IF member jurisdictions with one another. The database refers to bilateral tax treaties only. Multilateral agreements are not accounted for. Other tax-related agreements such as tax information exchange agreements are not counted. Only treaties in effect are counted.
Source: OECD Bilateral Tax Treaties Database.

StatLink https://stat.link/dt51a2

Figure 7.4. Average number of treaties, by region

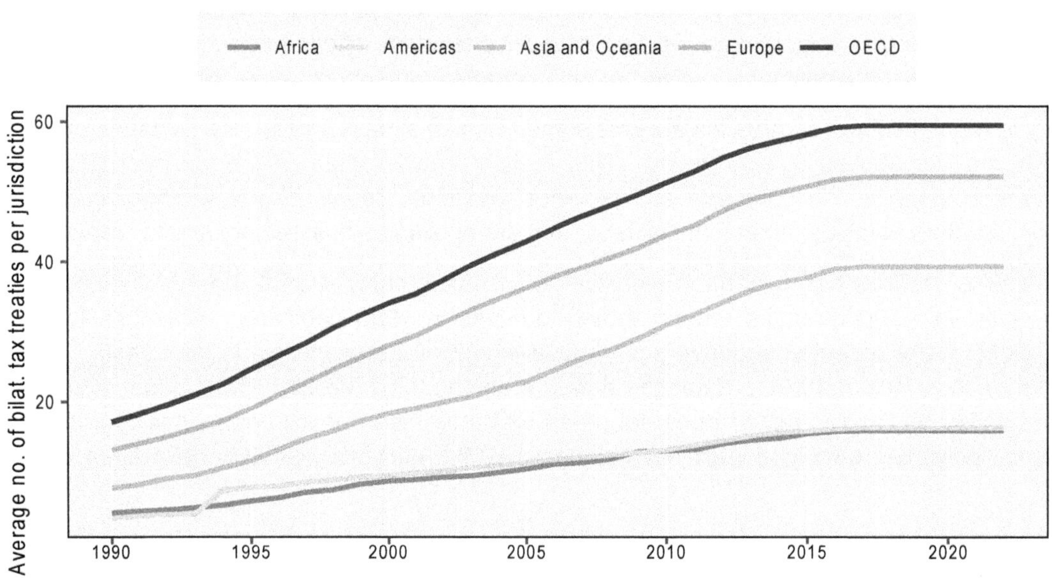

Note: Data are based on bilateral treaties reported by 131 IF member jurisdictions. The database refers to bilateral tax treaties only. Multilateral agreements are not accounted for. Other tax-related agreements such as tax information exchange agreements are not counted. Only treaties in effect are counted.
Source: OECD Bilateral Tax Treaties Database

StatLink https://stat.link/3it2p7

Figure 7.5. Average treaty-based withholding tax rates

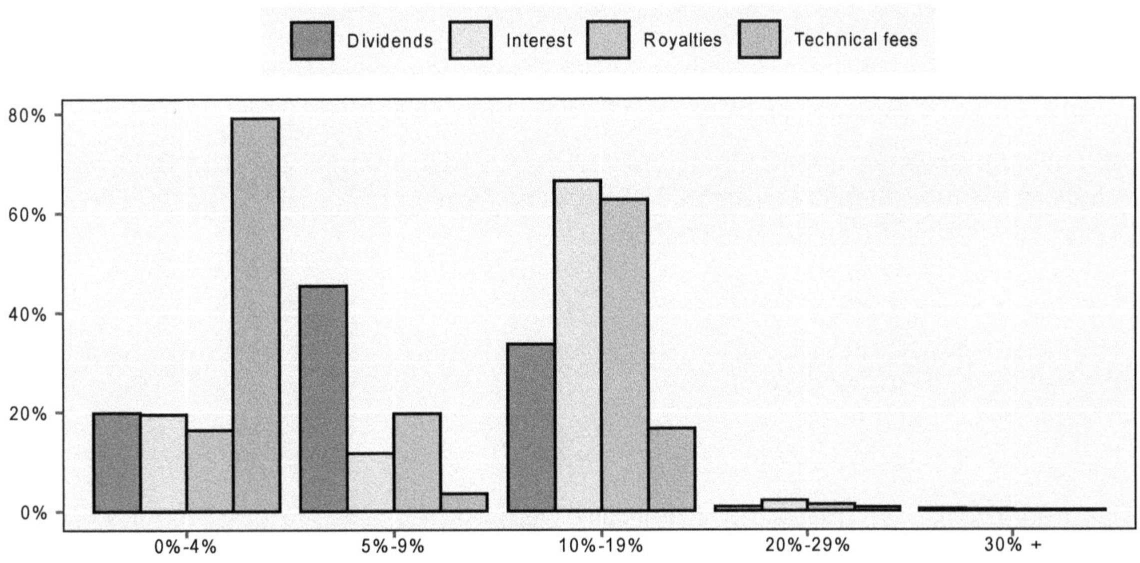

Note: Data are based on bilateral treaties reported by 131 IF member jurisdictions. The database refers to bilateral tax treaties only. Multilateral agreements are not accounted for. Other tax-related agreements such as tax information exchange agreements are not counted. Only treaties in effect are counted. For each of the categories of payment flows, existing treaties that do not specify the applicable withholding tax rate, and hence create missing values, are not included in this figure. Where a tax treaty provides for different rates for specified ownership percentages, this entry reflects the highest ownership percentage.
Source: OECD Bilateral Tax Treaties Data.

StatLink https://stat.link/385dg7

References

Auerbach, A., M. Devereux and H. Simpson (2008), "Taxing corporate income", https://www.nber.org/papers/w14494 (accessed on 18 February 2023). [1]

OECD (2015), *Measuring and Monitoring BEPS, Action 11 - 2015 Final Report*, OECD/G20 Base Erosion and Profit Shifting Project, OECD Publishing, Paris, https://doi.org/10.1787/9789264241343-en. [2]

Notes

[1] The "high income" and "low and middle income" jurisdiction groups are based on the World Bank classification, with the resulting split for the 119 jurisdictions covered: 49 high-income jurisdictions and 49 low- and middle-income jurisdictions. Low- and middle-income jurisdictions are grouped together due to the low number of low-income countries (two) in the dataset. Investment hubs constitute the third group. They are defined as jurisdictions with a total inward Foreign Direct Investment (FDI) position above 150% of gross domestic product (GDP) and include 21 jurisdictions.

[2] This means that the payments are not effectively connected with a permanent establishment in a jurisdiction applying a WHT.

[3] The analysis does not include updates or amendments to treaties. The data also do not include bilateral tax instruments that do not amend withholding taxes, such as taxpayer information exchange agreements.

www.ingramcontent.com/pod-product-compliance
Ingram Content Group UK Ltd.
Pitfield, Milton Keynes, MK11 3LW, UK
UKHW051507290926
15471UKWH00008B/1476

9 789264 732063